From Here To Forever

Mandelyn Kilroy

Copyright © 2013 Mandelyn Kilroy

All rights reserved.

To the people who have taught me love begins, love ends, and then love begins again.

CHAPTER ONE
Elizabeth

I have never, and will never, understand when someone says, "You need to pick up the pieces and move on from a relationship." Let's be totally, completely, one hundred percent brutally honest. It's not like you are actually ever going to move on. I mean if you genuinely loved that person (and I mean I can't eat, can't sleep, your sun rises and sets around them. Loved that person). You're just going to lie to yourself while ignoring your mangled and shattered heart. You hope, and you pray that tomorrow, when you wake up it won't hurt anymore. Even though it always does. You beg your heart to focus on anything other than the person who left you in ruins. You beg for an emotional lobotomy. So that maybe, just maybe, your thoughts of them and what was, will eventually stop consuming you every minute and every second of every day. Then if you're lucky, and don't hold your breath that this will ever actually happen. The pain may just be become a standard part of your daily routine. Allowing the ache in your chest where your heart once took up residence to become nothing more than a minor nuisance. Depressing thought, I know. Honestly though, you never truly move on from the love of your life, or the person you once considered your soul mate. You just learn the art of carefully managing the pain, or you curl up in a ball and die.

I had tried to curl up in a ball and die. It certainly had seemed like the easiest option. But my pain in the ass family would not hear of it. Instead, my over bearing grandmother had sent my brother, the prodigal child, to pull me out of my cocoon of pity and despair. Which is how I ended up sitting in the driver's seat of a moving van, pulling back into the town I swore I would never reside in again after I left for college. With a shattered heart and everything I owned packed in the back of the truck. Well, that was actually a lie. Very little of what I owned was in the back of the stupid truck. In fact, all that was back there were my books, clothes, and a few other personal items. The only furniture in the back of the truck was my desk and desk chair. I had been the person who purchased and paid for all of the furniture and decorations, so rightfully they were mine to take. But I just couldn't bring myself to take it all. It was covered in to many memories and guaranteed to grind my already shattered heart into a fine dust.

I rolled me eyes as I turned onto Main Street. It was like stepping back in time, untouched and unchanged for the last sixty years. Don't get me wrong. It is a perfectly lovely typical small town, population too small to matter. The dinner is just a cover for the gossip mill as it has been since it opened in 1951. Thanks to Ms. Patty, the owner and head gossip, everyone in town knows when you are in trouble long before you do. Yes, it's a perfectly lovely town if you like that sort of thing. It has been ten years since I graduate high school, and moved away for college. I swore the moment I got my acceptance letter to the University of Boston that I would never live anywhere but in the middle of a city again. Funny thing is ten years ago I had no idea I would be getting a divorce at twenty-eight. Nor was I aware that my prick of a husband would decide that if he couldn't live in the house, neither could I. Which I suppose is how the short and neater version of how I ended up here. Unhappy, alone, and leaving my heart in Boston.

Life didn't totally bend me over and screw me up the butt. After I graduate college with my degree in English and creative writing, I published my first novel. No, it was not as straight-forward as it sounds. There were a lot of struggles, sacrifices, and plenty of Ramen noodles. Regardless it paid off. My grandmother who has always been more of a mother to me than anyone else took one look at the check for my first book, and demanded I invest it. Any crazy Irish Catholic grandmother who was raised by a Great Depression survivor would demand exactly that. I knew it was coming before I even had the check in my hand. So I made her happy. I purchased a house directly behind hers. Which I have used as a rental property for the last eight years. A house that has conveniently been empty for the last two months. As well as an asset my soon to be dead, I mean ex-husband can't touch.

Don't sit there and applaud me or smile and think it's just so incredible that I have a place of my own to stay. In case you missed my above comment, the back door of my house faces my grandmother's back door. As in we share a back yard. As in she can walk twenty-five or fifty feet tops and be at my back door. Yes, both of our yards are fenced in, but that does not deter her in the slightest. Do not shake your head at me either. I'm sure you thinking "Oh how bad can your Nana be"? Well you have no idea. Don't get me wrong. I love her, I honestly do. The woman raised me, instilled morals, and taught me how to take care of myself. She is my biggest support, and my best friend. But she is a nosey, meddling, over bearing, her way or the highway, knows everything kind of woman. And did I mention Catholic? By Catholic I mean she goes to mass every morning, walks to church in blizzards, doesn't miss a day of church ever Catholic. While there is nothing wrong with this, it does mean that for the next six months to a year at least she is going to shake her head at me every time she sees me. Regardless of the fact that I did not want a divorce. I have still committed a mortal sin, which apparently is the worst kind of sin.

After eight hours in the car, I had never been so happy to see the house I had no desire to live in. Mostly because my ass had fallen asleep three hours ago. I had forgotten how long it took to get from Boston to the tiny town of Middleton an hour outside of Philadelphia. I had always found the town's name to be one gigantic irony. It was in the middle of bumble fuck nowhere, and full of simple middle people, who I fondly called simpletons growing up.

I pulled into the drive way, and right on queue there was my grandmother shaking her head in dismay. I fought the urge to roll my eyes. It would only make it worse. Eye rolling always started some lengthy speech about respect, and how disrespectful and snotty it was to roll my eyes at my elders. I couldn't help but smile. Just like the town, she hasn't changed a bit. For as long as I could remember, she has always had short platinum blond hair. She never left the house without at least a three inch heel, and I swear the woman has found the fountain of youth. She's going to be seventy-five next month and doesn't look a day over fifty. No, she has not gone under the knife. A little thing called white coat syndrome prevents her from even going to the doctor for a checkup without breaking out in hives from head to toe.

"Oh Izzy, I am so glad you finally got here. I was getting worried." She pulled me out of the truck before I had turned it off, pulling me into a fierce hug. Once again casually forgetting how much I hate the name Izzy. I had spent years trying to get her to call me Liz, or even my legal name Elizabeth. It has only made her call me Izzy more, and in the process let the terrible nick name rub off on other people.

"Hey Nana, sorry to worry you, the truck uses gas so much faster than my car. I had to stop twice to fill up." I didn't dare make eye contact. While it wasn't a complete lie, it wasn't anywhere near the entire truth.

"Elizabeth Breeze, don't you lie to me. You took the longest way possible, and I'm sure you pulled off at every rest stop along the way to smoke. Don't even deny it. You reek of cigarette smoke. You know those things are going to kill you one day. A long, slow, painful death." Do you remember when I told you that she was over bearing, and it was her way or the highway? You thought I was exaggerating correct? Well I wasn't.

"I know." I started, instantly regretting the two little words that had just fallen out of my mouth.

"Don't I know me missy, you sound just like your mother." They were venom filled words, and she knew damn right well that sentence was the nastiest punishment she could dole out. She only dropped that bomb when I had seriously pissed her off. There was never anything productive to say back to that statement. Anything other than silence would only result in her hand print across my cheek.

"So did the tenets leave a mess? Does the house need a lot of work?" I already knew the answer. I asked to change the subject before she threw out anymore way below the belt remarks.

"No darling, it's in fine shape. But I was thinking now that you will be living here, maybe it could use some redecorating?" She turned and marched into the front door. I sighed knowing that the tenets had repainted the house room by room over the past few years. They were a young couple just married when they had moved in. Their first two children had been conceived in this house, as well as called it home their entire lives. It wasn't until she became pregnant with her third that they decided they had to move, and finally purchase their first home. I had been sad to see them go. I was even sadder now that I apparently needed to re-paint every room in my two story three bedroom cape cod. I walked in the front door and held my breath. With the exception of paint samples taped to every wall, and carpet and hardwood samples scattered on the floors the house looked like it had been uninhabited for the last eight years.

"Nan, look I know you mean well, but can I get settled in before we start a huge project?" I was willing to get down on my knees and beg her. Wven I could hear the desperation dripping off of my voice.

She sighed, and looked at me like I was a five year old child who didn't understand why she couldn't have chocolate ice cream for dinner. "No darling, it will be easier to do when the house is empty. There is less to move that way. Besides, the handy man is going to be here any minute." Hands on her hips, daring me to argue with her. It's moments like this when I have no idea how either one of us made it out of my teenage years alive. I threw my hands up in defeat, this was a pointless fight.

"Nan, you know what? You're right. Can we start in my office and bedroom? Those are the rooms I will use most, and I need them to be calming." They were also the only two rooms I had any desire to unpack and set up. I had been looking forward to doing it tonight. My original thought had been it would distract me from not being in the house I called home. She grabbed my hand and dragged me up the stairs, excitement radiating from every pore in her body. Let me make one thing clear. She was only taking me along as a formality. She already had the paint colors, and the flooring picked out. She knew it would piss me off if she came right out and admitted that. Just like we both knew I'd play along. I'd look at the colors before letting her pick what she wanted anyway. It was easier that way. We had mastered this game years ago. I was saved by the doorbell ten long minutes later. At that exact moment, I was debating decapitating myself with the office window.

"Darling, that will be the handy man. You go let him in while I finish picking out the paint color for the kitchen." She waved her hand in the direction of the front door. I gladly sprinted away from her, and the paint color fight in the office. I was going to need to find some sort of job to get me out of the house and fast. Not because I needed money. Well, truthfully I might with the way she is planning on re-doing my house. No, I needed to get some type of job so I was not sitting fifty-feet away from her house twenty-four hours a day. I threw open the front door and stopped dead in my tracks. The air rushing out of my lungs in pure shock. I would know the piercing blue eyes staring back at me anywhere. I almost melted as his all too familiar slow smile crept across his lips. The same lips that could once make me melt, with just the thought of them on mine. Handy man my ass. My grandmother was up to no good, and I had only been back in town for all of thirty minutes. If this trip down memory lane was going to spend any amount of time in this house, under the false pretenses of a handy man, I was going to turn right around and head back to Boston. A box under a bridge would be better than re-opening that chapter of my life. Clearly Nan had missed that memo. I think she would have casually missed it even if I had issued it on a billboard.

"I heard you were back in town Pige." His voice sent a shudder down my spine. I hated my body for still responding to his voice even after all this time.

"Yeah Brandon, I got back here about an hour ago, and was promptly informed that I couldn't even move my bed in and go to sleep." I rolled my eyes, trying desperately to come off nonchalant.

I didn't want him to know his presence had any effect on me.

"Yeah Nan called me last week. She said something about painting the entire house and putting in new flooring?" He leaned against the door frame. I hadn't moved to let him in yet. I still wasn't sure I was going to let him in period.

"A week ago! Are you kidding me? I hadn't even decided I was coming back here a week ago. In fact, I hadn't been informed until forty-eight hours ago that I was coming back here." I was now thoroughly pissed. I could understand her rushing out after my brother got to Boston. If she did this once my ex had reported back that I had to be out of my home in forty-eight hours, then I could understand her picking up paint and flooring samples. If she had done that, I would have accepted it as her way of trying to give me the fresh start she thinks I need. A week ago though?! That means that little witch in my kitchen has been planning this since she found out a month ago I was getting a divorce. Yes, that's right today is exactly one months since my asshole husband rolled over after his Monday morning before work sex and told me he wanted a divorce. Brandon's laughter snapped me out of the memories I wasn't ready to let haunt me today. I saved that pleasure for when I tossed and turned at night, unable to sleep without the light snoring beside me. The snoring I had grown so accustom to. I looked up and couldn't help but smile. Brandon was doubled over clutching his stomach as his laughter erupted from deep within his soul. His chestnut hair fell into his eyes, and for just a moment I was sixteen again, sitting on my grandmother's front steps, talking until the sun rose.

"Some things never change doll. Now let's see what we can do about getting your bedroom started. So you can sleep in your own bed before the end of the week." He took a step towards me. I quickly stepped back. Close proximately to Brandon was not something I wanted to happen, ever again. Been there, done that, and it had ended badly. I almost laughed at the irony of this situation. The first person to ever break my heart and the same person who unknowingly pushed me to seek comfort in my husband's arms was now standing on my front steps, and a key player in my grandmother's grand plan of a fresh start, and finding comfort in the wake of my husband breaking my heart. The universe has a seriously sick sense of humor.

I stepped aside pointing to the kitchen. "She is in there and has grandiose plans. In fact, regardless of what she tells you, she has had everything picked out long before she called you." I watched him chuckle as he walked down the hall. My breath caught in my throat as his hips swayed with each step, pulling his jeans a little tighter across his back side. My god time has been good to that boy. The thought slipped out before I had time to shut it down. I mentally punched myself, and refused to join them in the kitchen. Instead, I slipped out the front door, pulling a cigarette out of my back pocket, before trying to find a safe place to hide. My name is Elizabeth or Izzy when my grandmother isn't mad at me, and I am currently hiding in my own bush to smoke a cigarette. Just like I am sixteen and afraid of getting caught. This is why I said I was never moving back home. This and the devilishly sexy handy man standing somewhere in my house, whom I swore I would hate for the rest of my life. In fact, he was the reason I was at the bar I was at the night I met Jonathan, my soon to be ex-husband. So in all honesty I genuinely should hate Brandon even more right now.

I was going to have to put the immense hatred I couldn't seem to muster on the back burner until he was done my house. Then and only then would I give my emotions free rein to wage and no holds bar hatred war against him. I felt my phone vibrate in my bra. Yes, I keep my phone in my bra, don't judge me. I breathed a sigh of relief when I saw it was my best friend.

"Hey, Madison." I whispered.

"So you really are back. Hiding in the bush smoking already? That has to be a new world record." She joked as I laughed along with her. There was a reason we had been best friends since Kindergarden.

"Yes, and you will never guess who is in my damn house." I hissed.

"Brandon, yeah I know. I was going to warn you. But in all honesty I decided it was going to be a hell of a lot funnier to let you be surprised. So, how long until you throw him against the wall and have your way with him?" Mel frankly asked. It was one thing I had always loved about the girl she didn't sugar coat shit. However, she could not be any more wrong with her previous statement.

"I'm not. I hate him remember?" I shot back, no longer whispering, which was going to put me at a much higher risk of getting caught.

"Yeah, if you want to call it that. You hate him just like I am having an affair with Prince Harry. Keep lying to yourself, Iz. Listen the baby is screaming I will call you tomorrow, maybe we can grab lunch." The line went dead before I could protest, or tell her no.

"You know you don't have to hide in the bush. Nan only gives you shit about smoking because you let her." Brandon parted the bush, a cigarette dangled from his lips. I rolled my eyes and climbed out of the bush, glancing over my shoulder at the front door before lighting a second one.

"So everything is all sorted out?" It was generic question; I needed to keep the small talk to a minimum. If he wasn't responsible for making my house look lovely, I wouldn't bother to speak to him at all.

"Yeah your room will be done by tomorrow night. I'm going to go pick up the paint, and get that painted today. That way I can lay the floor tomorrow." He smiled that still managed to make me ever so slightly weak in the knees.

"Thanks Bran, I really appreciate it." I smile my first genuine smile since I don't know how long. He leaned forward catching my off guard.

"Just between me and you, I'd get a new bed before you come home and find yours gone. Something about a fresh start?" His breath hit my cheek, and I closed my eyes. For just a moment, I let myself get lost in his musky rich scent.

"Thanks for acting like you haven't already herd eight different versions of the truth. Don't worry I left most of the furniture there for him to deal with. I actually ordered everything online before I left Boston. It is going to be delivered at five tonight." We both shared the same knowing smile, over how Nan worked.

"Then I'll set your bed up in the living room before I leave tonight." He smiled as he got in his truck. I wanted to protest, but it was pointless. He would just get Nan on his side. That was always a battle I was sure to lose. This wasn't my first go around, with Brandon's unique technique for getting his way with me. Don't even let your mind go there. He never used my grandmother to let me let him get his way with me sexually. I'm shaking my head at you. And before you go there that was not me admitting Brandon and I have ever done anything sexual. What happened with Brandon and me is in the past, and that is where I intend to leave it. I may even succeed as soon as he is done with my house. That is as long as Nan and Madison stay the hell out of it. Which we both know isn't going to happen. So keep your pants on because soon enough I am going to rehash the history of Brandon and me. My grandmother and her meddling are going to be the death of me, and she may have gone too far this time. Just for the record.

CHAPTER TWO
Brandon

I put the car in park just around the corner from Pigeon's house, willing my body to relax. I was shaking uncontrollably with excitement over Pige finally coming home. I knew it was only because her world had just come crashing down around her. I should feel ashamed for being happy when she is so destroyed. But I am not, not even close.

I had stood there in shock when the door opened earlier. I pinched myself just to be sure I wasn't dreaming up the girl standing in front of me. I had tried not to hope when Nan hired me to re-model the house Pige owned, that maybe I would at least get to hear Pigeon's voice at some point in time. Yes, I still call her Nan. I have been doing it since kindergarten. In all honestly most days, I can't even remember her real name. But I had no idea there would be any chance Pige would actually be here. Let alone standing in the doorway the day the renovation started. I can't believe I had not stopped to consider it after Nan discreetly pulled me aside to fill me in that Pige was getting a divorce. Pige had never wanted to spend her life in this small tow. So why would she come back? A hell of a lot more must have gone down in Boston then Nan let on.

"How can I write if I don't have any real life experience? I mean how much can you grow in a town that you can drive across in less than five minutes?" She had asked me the day she got her acceptance letter to Boston University. She hadn't told anyone she was even applying there. It was also the same day the future I hadn't realized I wanted came crashing down around me. I knew as I had watched her pack eighteen years of memories into the trunk of her Honda Civic the night before she left for college that she had no plans of ever living in this town again. Boston, New York, Philadelphia, even Los Angeles were where she was going to spend the rest of her life. Places I couldn't imagine living. So to be entirely honest after I realized she wasn't an illusion. I almost shit a brick over the fact hat Pigeon was actually standing in front of me with a moving van parked in the driveway. Just as all my dreams came rushing back.

I can't lie the girl looked like hell. The girl I once knew and loved had been a feisty little creature so full of life. She had creativity seeping from her pores. The girl blocking the doorway was a shell of whom she used to be. The hazel eyes that could paralyze me no longer sparkled with hints of trouble, and excitement. Instead, the life in them had slowly faded away. Taking with them the flecks of grey and purple that used to captivate me. They no longer sparkled with promise. Her gorgeous, chocolate cherry hair, that always took my breath away, as she lay sleeping with it strewn across the pillow case, or my chest. It was a dull mess piled on the top of her head, clearly unwashed for longer than I wanted to imagine. She had always been thin. But my god did she have a body that could bring you to your knees in high school. A tight little bump on her back side, a chest that put Playboy bunnies to shame, her toned flat little tummy, and legs that went on for days. The legs had been the most dangerous part of Pige's body in high school. The second she wrapped them around my waist we both knew she was going to get her way. Her body had disappeared, it was no longer toned, or anything that could be considered skinny. Pige looked like she had not eaten in weeks. I actually was concerned that she had become anorexic. Even thru her baggy t-shirt I could tell that her stomach was no longer flat, it was actually sunken in. Much like her eyes and cheeks. She looked like a bag of bone being held up by the door frame.

I stopped caring about the re-model, and that Nan was probably somewhere in the house, not so patiently waiting for me. All I cared about was the devastated person in front of me. I wanted to wrap the girl I once loved up my arms. Keep her safe from whatever had caused her to give up living. I wanted nothing more than to force fed her a pizza, cheese fries, and anything else fatty I could get in her body. Hell, if she asked I'd drive the nearly three hours round trip to Pat's in Philadelphia to get her a dozen cheese steaks. She may not be around for long, and under no circumstances could I let myself hope that she was here for good. But she was here now, and I was going to do everything in my power to breathe some life back into her. All I needed to do now was come up with a way to do it without shattering my own heart again. I knew the second her angelic voice escaped her lips, she was going to break my heart again. I couldn't bring myself to walk away again, like I had all those years ago. Not when life had finally just been breathed into my heart by her presence. Causing it to beat for the first time in eight years.

I threw the car in drive, full of newly discovered enthusiasm. I could not wait to go back to her house so I could put operation win her back into motion. I was not going to let her walk out of my life again. Not without one hell of a fight, a battle eight years in the making.

CHAPTER THREE
Elizabeth

Brandon has been painting up stairs for the last two hours. I have no idea why this process takes so long. I mean seriously all four walls are being painted the same color. Don't bother to ask me what color it is. If you recall I was not under any circumstances permitted to have a say in the paint colors. I heard his footsteps echo down the hall starting down the stairs.

"Hey Pige, I was ordered to make sure you eat. You know Nan, she is worries you're going to curl up in a ball and die. So, how about we split a pizza and maybe a six pack?" He sat down across from me on the floor, pushing my laptop shut with his foot in an attempt to get my attention.

"Yeah, the curling up in a ball thing didn't work out to well. That's how I ended up back here." I sighed waiving my hand around , motioning to the house around me. "And sure I'd love pizza, and a beer. I'll buy. Where do you want to go?" I asked pushing my computer aside. It was easier to just give in. Just like going out to eat was a million times easier than sitting on my floor sharing a pizza. Not to mention I could get rid of him faster. Besides if I refused dinner he would just call Nan and she would come over and force feed me. I finally looked up meeting his eyes, looking away just as fast. I could not handle the pity the filled them. I knew just as well as he did the girl he knew in high school, was not the kind of girl who let a relationship destroy her. If only he knew how wrong he had been about me even back then. The broken heart he induced without even realizing it had almost killed me.

"Pizzas and beer are going to be here in about five minutes Pige." He said shrugging his shoulders, unashamed of his omission. Making it abundantly clear I had no choice about the next hour of my evening. "It's kind of a nice night out. Plus there is an oversized hammock out back. Want to eat out there? It's more comfortable than this floor." He smiled at me, but his eyes still held the pity I was desperately trying to avoid at all costs.

"Wait, I'm sorry they deliver beer?" I am so confused. I know damn right well you couldn't get beer delivered. If that was possible I never would have left my house during my wallowing stint.

"Small town, remember Pige? Everyone knows everyone. Which means that Sammy's pizza knows I'm old enough to legally buy beer, because I pick up a six pack from them at least once a week. So yes, they will deliver it with my pizza. My god girl you have clearly forgotten how a small town works. My guess would be you have lived in that big city for far too long." He stood up tussling my hair on the way to the front door. "Oh and Pige, dinner is on me, Get your ass out back, or I'm not sharing," His laughter echoing back into the living room. The distantly familiar sound making me oddly comfortable, and extremely uncomfortable at the same time.

I sighed, standing up and walking towards the back door. I am a girl on a mission. Eat, small talk, and be in bed in less than an hour. So the sooner we eat, the sooner I can go back to my misery.

From here to forever

My reflection in the microwave stopped me dead in my tracks. I suddenly understood everyone's concern about me eating. I looked like death. It was the first time I had acknowledged my appearance in a month. My chestnut hair, which normally hung straight and grazed the top of my breasts, was piled on top of my head. In what can only be described as a greasy rat's nest. The bags under my eyes would put the bag lady in Central Park to shame. Tomorrow I was going to get up, take a long shower, and put on clean clothes. I can't honestly remember if I have done any of thee above it in the last month. Can't remember or don't want to admit that I haven't, it's all the same at the end of the day. Either way I smelled like a dump. I had to stop ignoring my basic needs.

"Yeah Pige you look like complete shit." Brandon said in my ear jerking me back to the present. "Let's eat" He held up the pizza and beer, nodding towards the open back door. He walked out not bothering to see if I followed. The smell of hot cheese and sauce assaulted me causing my stomach to growl in response. I quickly walked to the back door, leaning against the door frame.

I stood watching him climb into the hammock sitting cross legged at one end, waiting for me to climb in on the other side. We had mastered this technique years ago. I walked across the yard towards the hammock. Quickly climbing in and passing him a beer while opening one for myself. Taking a long swig, while discovering I was unsure of what to say next. Instead of saying anything I sat quietly peeling the label off of my beer and picking at the crust of my pizza. I knew he had already heard some version of what had conspired in Boston. I desperately needed to know what he had been told. Yet I couldn't bring myself to ask for fear of just how much the truth had been stretched. Plus if I ask him then you see I am forced to tell him the truth. I don't think I have truly told anyone the complete truth yet. Hell, I haven't even admitted the whole truth to myself yet. By refusing to talk about it I am leaving everyone with a lot of unanswered questions. Unanswered questions that are only adding fuel to the rumor mill fire.

"Pigeon, if you don't want to talk about it, then don't. You should know me well enough to know I don't listen to the rumors. Just like I do not participate in spreading them. The only thing I know is what Nan told me." He slid his finger under my chin gently forcing me to look up from my lap, and into his eyes. " And from the looks of you darling, she was being very modest in her telling." A single tear slipped past my lashes, and slid down my cheek, finally, coming to rest on the tip of his thumb.

"Well, are you going to tell me what she said? Or are you going to keep me guessing?" My voice quivered as I continued fighting back the sob building in my chest. His thumb gently caressed my check in a slow circle. I tilted my head into his hand. Unaware of just how much I needed to be comforted.

"Aw hell Pige, it doesn't really matter. What does matter is you are sitting here fighting back the tears you don't deserve to be crying. You are clearly in a living hell right now. So, why don't you tell me what happened? Before I end up in Boston beating the life out of that piece of shit asshole who made you cry." Brandon slid the pizza box to the ground next to us, pulling me against him in a fierce hug. It was exactly what I didn't know I needed. I shifted against him until my entire body was curled into his lap. For the first time in a month, I didn't feel completely and utterly alone. I pressed my face into his chest, finally, letting the damn break. I hadn't cried when Jonathan told me he wanted a divorce. I hadn't cried as he packed his suitcase into the trunk of the car. The same suitcase he had packed days in advance. Hell I didn't even shed a single tear when I closed my front door for the last time earlier today. I had held it all in until this very minute.

From here to forever

Thankfully, Brandon didn't say a word. Just like he didn't try to stop me, or slow the tears. Instead, he held me tightly to his chest, rocking the hammock gently letting me cry until there were no tears left. I don't know how long we sat there with only the sound of my sobs. Just like I don't know how long he stroked my hair after I was finished crying.

Finally, lifting my head from his chest, I started talking. "Brandon, I'm…" He pressed his fingers to my lips silencing me.

"Don't you dare say you are sorry. You have nothing to be sorry for. I will not tolerate you apologizing, for finally purging. Do you understand me?" I couldn't help but smile slightly. He had always hated how the first words out of my mouth anytime I got emotional were I'm sorry. I held up my hands in frustration as he took his hand away.

"Okay fine, I don't owe you an apology, but I owe you some sort of explanation." I sighed holding my hands up to stop him from arguing. The idea of explaining anything was exhausting. Let alone actually laying everything out there.

"Only if you want to. You clearly don't look like you are emotionally ready to drag it all out of the closet tonight." He slid my beer back into my hands and set the pizza back on the hammock. "How about you tell me when you are ready? In the meantime, you eat. I can tell just by looking at you that eating is a concept you have neglected over the last month." He pushed the box into my lap, nodding his head at the pizza in front of me. I picked up a piece, not wanting to upset the person who had kindly just let me soak his shirt. He took a long drag of his beer and just like that the conversation was closed.

"Bran, thanks for understanding." I mustered up a small sad smile. "So what color is my room?" I didn't need anymore emotional break downs tonight. So, changing the subject to paint color was a safe bet. Brandon's eyes went wide staring at me like I had suddenly sprouted three heads. His beer bottle hung in the air inches from his lips. His brow wrinkled as utter shock played across his face.

"You don't know what color your room is? I have been up there painting all afternoon, and you don't know what color it is. Aw, damn Pige, I hope that's a joke cause I really don't want to spend all day tomorrow repainting it." I could feel myself melting at his almost nonexistent southern drawl.

"Brandon you have you met my grandmother correct? If you do remember you told me earlier that she planned on re-doing my house over a week ago, only to spring it on me today. So she is the one who picked out the flooring, and all of the paint colors darling. Not me." I said with a sigh, letting the truth slowly sink in. As his laughter started I closed my eyes, letting the sound wash over me. His laughter had always been one of my favorite sounds. There was just something about how it started out light and gradually transformed into a deep rich hearty laugh that I swear comes from the very tips of his toes.

"Your room is a very pale purple, and tomorrow we will go over all of the other colors she has picked out. If you don't like any of them or your room I will change it, and personally deal with Nan." He was so serious and eager to please. His eyes search my face, trying to read my reaction.

"No, no. Purple will be perfect. I prefer calming colors in my bedroom anyway. I had attempted to paint the bedroom in Boston a grayish light purple, but Jonathan has vetoed it." I said, kicking myself the moment his name left my lips. Not to mention vetoed had been a lie. The bedroom paint color fight had turned into more of a hostile takeover.

"What a douche." I could tell the words had just fallen out of his mouth. His eyes got wide revealing he immediately regretted the slip. His face tinted with eight different shades of embarrassed red. He opened his mouth, and before he could apologize I cut him off.

"Could not have said it better myself." I laughed opening my second beer. Something I was going to regret in the morning, when I woke up with a terrible head ache. I tipped the bottle to my lips and chugged it, attempting to wash away the memories that were suffocating me.

CHAPTER FOUR
Brandon

I lay next to the mattress on the floor. A pathetic make shift bed, watching Pige sleep. I should get up and walk away. Hell, I should be running as fast as I can in the other direction. I should go home and take a cold shower. What I honestly should have done was answered my phone two hours ago. When Candice text massaged me for the first time, instead of standing her up. If I had gone that route a cold shower would be the last thing I needed. Instead, I would be showering to wash Candice's scent off of me before it turned my stomach. I of cours, being the fucking masochist I am, didn't leave. I ignored my phone, and I lay on the floor, fighting the urge to climb in next to Pige. There is nothing I want more than to be selfish and hold her all night long.

   A stray strand of hair lay across her forehead. I timidly reached out a finger retracting before it reached her face. Holding her while she had cried earlier had been dangerous enough. I had spent too many god damn years locking down the heartache and resentment I felt towards her. I couldn't let her sweep back into my life and open Pandora's box again. Another deep sigh of want slipped past my lips as she whimpered in her sleep. Her dark chocolate hair splayed against her pale skin. I wanted nothing more than to gently brush it off her face. She was beautiful, even when she was at her absolute worst. In fact, right now with her hair all a mess and a tear-streaked face, I would swear she had never looked more stunning. It took my breath away. I had forgotten what a lightweight she was. I figured she had built up a tolerance during college, and could handle more than one beer. I had been so very, very wrong. I was still sitting here on the floor, two hours after I put her to bed because it was the only way I could guarantee that I wouldn't drive to Boston and beat the living shit out of her piece of shit, worthless ex-husband.

I already knew that there was no way in hell tomorrow morning she would remember what she told me after she finished her second beer. So I had until she woke up to suppress and contain my anger over it. I had wanted to kill him as she lay against my chest sobbing. But after she had started rambling about him and their marriage, I swear on everything holy I was lining up an alibi in my head. I couldn't sit there and watch her cry, so I pulled her into my arms, trying to comfort her as best I could. In the end, I just held her for over an hour, gently swaying back and forth. While biting my tongue and fighting the urge to say something. I had foolishly thought that she was done crying for the night. Well I clearly had forgotten that alcohol makes her extremely emotional.

It was shortly after she finished her second beer and her first slice of pizza, when the drunken rambling started. That was my first crucial mistake of the evening. Letting her drink on an almost empty stomach. She threw herself out of the hammock in the most ungraceful dismount I have ever had the joy of witnessing. If falling out of a hammock was an Olympic sport she would have won the gold medal. She landed face first in the dirt. Her long legs were still tangled in the hammock as well as mine. I watched her flop around like a fish out of water as I fought desperately against the urge to laugh. I finally let my pity on the drunken girl take over. I grabbed her legs and freed them, laying them on the ground next to her. Narrowly missing a foot to the side of my head. She of course, couldn't just stand up like a normal person. No, instead she army crawled away from the offending hammock before using a tree trunk to pull herself up. She stayed upright for all of five seconds before falling into a bush. A bush might I add that is no longer taking up residence in her back yard. I didn't bother to get out the hammock to help her. Instead I opened my third beer, and watched her rip the bush out of the ground, hurling it across the yard for good measure. I knew that before she was done, she was going to fall into the hole she had just created.

Look, I get it okay. Me sitting back and watching her stumble around the back yard makes me look like a cold heartless bastard. I'm not. I swear. You just don't know the stubborn little vixen like I do. If I stood up and attempted to help her while she is this wound up, we would both end up in jail again. Yes, I said again. Trust me. She would punch me in the face. Then I would throw her over my shoulder, carry her out front, and hose her off. Which would end up in her attempting to fight me off and probably scream rape so one of the neighbors would call the police. By the time they got there, I would be holding her down in a pitiful attempt to protect my boys, and we would both get arrested. Yes, that has happened in the past, more than once. I don't know about you, but I seriously don't have time for that side trip this evening. Which is why I just sat back and waited. I knew she was going to explode any second, and if I didn't make any sudden movements she would get it all out, calm down, and then just about pass out so I could carry her to the safety of her bed. She truly is like a scared wild animal when she gets like this.

" The fucking asshole." She finally screamed as she kicked the bush. "You know what Brandon, you're right. He is a douche bag.

Did you know that he wanted me to give up writing so I could be barefoot and pregnant? Yup, he did. He wanted me to give up what I love so I could become some baby-making machine. Well clearly that didn't happen." She started to remove her shirt only to get stuck with it half way off.

"Pige, what the hell are you doing?" I chuckled as she stumbled around blind.

" Trying to show you my stretch mark free, flat stomach." She mumbled. I finally stood up, and walked over to help her. The last thing I needed was a trip to the emergency room tonight because she knocked herself out trying to take her shirt off. I walked the five feet separating us just as she started to cry again. " I couldn't give up my writing." She sobbed as I pulled down her shirt.

"I know Pige. That's all you ever wanted." I quietly responded, hoping it would soothe her in some way. It didn't. Her open palm connected with the side of my face. Like I said earlier, it's easier to sit back and let her work it all out without interfering.

"No, you dick, I couldn't give up my writing because I can't have children." She slumped down in the ground, sticking her head between her knees. My knees started to buckle, at her omissions. I reached out for the oak tree to steady myself. It took every ounce of strength not to sink down next to her on the ground. I could feel my heart shattering for her as the truth finally dawned on me. It was my fault she couldn't have children. I stumbled backwards, sinking into the hammock. I had spent the last ten years trying to forget about the unplanned pregnancy that had the potential to ruin her life.

Neither of us had realized she was pregnant, she was on the pill, and we thought that it was enough to protect us. We were wrong. I will never forget the sound of her voice when she climbed thru my window a little after midnight.

"Brandon, Brandon wake up something is wrong." She

whispered her voice laced with pain. I opened my eyes just as she collapsed on my floor withering in pain. I didn't bother to think, and I screamed for my mom. I am sure I gave her and my dad a heart attack when they came racing in my room. I was on the floor holding Pige's head in my lap as blood soaked thru her sweatpants. My mother being the most extraordinary person in the world instantly ordered me to get dressed, while she told my dad to pick Pige up and carry her to the car. I raced down the stairs after them praying that she would be okay. It was the longest ten-minute car ride of my life. My mother called her grandmother on the way to the hospital. I knew things were bad when Nan walked in two minutes behind us still in her pajamas, hair not done, and no makeup on. I watched my mother and Nan talk quietly in the corner. I was helpless, and they wouldn't let us back to see her. Finally after what felt like a lifetime the doctors came out and spoke to us.

"Were any of you aware that she was pregnant?" He asked solemnly. Everyone looked at me in shock. Obviously I hadn't advertised that we were having sex.

"No, she just had her period two weeks ago. She can't be pregnant." I was shaking with fear. There was no way she could be pregnant. We kept track of her periods just to be safe, she had never been a day late since we started having sex.

"I am very sorry to tell you all, but Elizabeth was three months pregnant. She however, had a utopia pregnancy. Which miscarried earlier this evening. In the process it ruptured her fallopian tube. We have stopped the bleeding, as well as made sure all of the miscarriage has passed. However, she sustained severe damage to her fallopian tube and uterus, all of it is irrevocable." My mother and her grandmother were crying before he finished. I was in shock, and my brain as well as the rest of my body went numb.

"How will this affect her chances of conceiving later in life?"

My mother asked thru her sobs. My father stood with his arms around both women. I was frozen in place.

"She will have a much harder time conceiving. There is a very strong possibility that she may not be able to conceive." He turned towards me. " Son she is asking for you." I turned and almost sprinted down the hallway. I needed to see her. I walked into her room, and my heart stopped. She was laying with her back to me. Her shoulder shook with the silent sobs I already knew were escaping her lips. I crossed the room in three strides and slide into bed behind her. She turned and buried her head in my chest. Where we lay and mourned the loss, hers much greater than mine.

No one ever spoke of it after that night. Until just now when she confirmed my greatest fear. I looked up, finally getting my emotions under control enough to put my mask back in place. She was lying in a ball on the ground, her eyes were half closed, and her breathing was quickly becoming shallow. I stood up, taking a careful step, making sure that I was steady. I walked over to her squatting down and picking her up. I cradled her gently against my body, carrying her into bed.

The screen on my cell phone lit up again with another text message from Candice. She had text messaged me ten times in the last few hours. I was supposed to meet her for dinner and drinks tonight. Actually I was supposed to meet her about ten minutes before Pige blurted out that she couldn't have children. I should be a gentleman and text message her back. But she should also not be a crazy stage-five clinger. If I text messaged her then she would call to chew me out. Which I didn't have time for. I was far to comfortable sitting on the floor watching Pigeon sleep. Even though my butt had gone numb an hour ago.

The screen on my phone told me it was after midnight, and I had to be back here in a few hours. I wanted nothing more than to climb into bed next to her and spend the rest of the night holding her. Which meant it was time to walk away and go home. I pulled the blanket back up over her before I backed out of her living room. Quickly making sure the back door was locked before locking the front door and closing it behind me. I leaned my head against her door. I was in too deep, and she had only been here for less than twenty-four hours.

CHAPTER FIVE
Elizabeth

I threw myself awake with a frantic jolt. My breath caught in my throat, as my lung burned desperate from oxygen. Gasping for air in a pitiful attempt to calm the panic attack. I let my eyes adjust to the dark taking in my surroundings. As the realization that I had just woken up from sleeping in the living room of my house in Middleton sunk in. The panic attack receded. I am still fully clothed, and much to my dismay moving here and the divorce were sadly not just a terrible dream. Of course, they were actually a nightmare. But not the kind of nightmare I could wake up from. This has become my standard morning routine, or to be honest when I ever wake up. Which truthfully wasn't often, because sleep has become a foreign concept. This lovely trend started the day my husband left me. Let's be honest that's when everything shitty started.

    I had watched Jonathan load his suitcases into the trunk of car from the bedroom window. Wrapped in my twelve hundred thread count Egyptian cotton sheets. After his car backed down the driveway I had curled up in a ball fully intending to never move again. I let the numbness over take me and lull me into an unrestful sleep.

I woke up hours later in a pitch-black room, alone and in a panic. Some part of me (Ok it was a tremendously large part of me, if I'm being honest) had hoped I would wake up and discover that it had all been a nightmare. I threw my self at his closet, needing my prayers to be answered. Needing to find his clothes still hanging there. I held my breath waiting for him to walk into the room and ask me what the hell I was doing. It never happened his clothes were gone. He was never going to walk back thru the bedroom door. He was never going to pull me against him in bed. Or mumble about what was going on at work into my hair as he drifted off to sleep. I spent the rest of the night curled up in the corner of his closet, suffocated by my inability to cry. I had desperately wanted to cry, to give into the sorrow that was eating me alive. I knew it would provide some sense of relief. It would ease the ache deep within my soul that was overtaking me. Much like high tide on a full moon over took the shore. If I could have just cried maybe the pain would recede, maybe my heart wouldn't feel like it was ready to explode from the unbearable pain.

No, I hadn't been able to cry. I wasn't that lucky. Instead, I had let the suffocating pain over take me from the inside out. That was until last night. Stupid Brandon, and his stupid understanding eyes. His silence filled with the acceptance that I was broken. He didn't pass judgment or attempt to fix me. No, instead he had broken the damn releasing the flood of tears I had grown accustom to keeping locked up.

I glanced at my cell phone screen trying to distract myself from thoughts of last night, discovering it was eight am. I couldn't remember what time I had fallen asleep. But for the first time in a month I felt rested. As well as very, very empty. That is the thing about letting the damn break, and letting the pain out. Once it is gone there is nothing left to replace it, but emptiness. The pain I can deal with, I can manage it. Keep my self-distracted so it doesn't consume me. Yes, I know I haven't exactly been doing a exceptionally good job of that recently. But I was going to start managing it. I swear. I was going to start getting up everyday and showering, I was going to start working on my next book. In fact, I had started working on it last night. Ok so I wrote five words. But it was a start.

But now I was empty. Which might I add is a feeling no one can manage. There is nothing left to manage once the emptiness has set in. There was no more pain to ignore, no more tears to hold back. The only option left was to get up and attempt to continue on. To try to find things to fill the void. I would much rather be consumed with pain, and plaster a fake smile across my face, then suffer with this bullshit.

I sighed pushing myself off of the mattress. I had decided last night this morning I was going to attempt to look human again. Attempt being the key word in that statement. Now was as good of a time as ever. Besides if I put it off any longer I was never going to get off this mattress. What I actually wanted was a cup of coffee, and a bagel. However, there was no food in my house. My coffee maker was still packed in the back of the truck, and there is no way in hell I am going to walk into the dinner looking like I look. The rumors would be flying before my cup of coffee was poured. While no one in this town will admit it, I honestly think that there is a gossip phone tree. You know like those call lists they have for school crap. If you are shaking your head in confusion let me break it down for you.

When good gossip hits the dinner. Who the hell am I kidding when any gossip finds it's way to the dinner. Ms. Patty calls two people and tells them the gossip. These two people then have two more people. Those two people call two more, and so on and so on. Of course, this gossip phone tree also becomes like whisper down the lane. If I walked into the dinner, Ms. Patty's call would sound something like.

" Oh my god girl you will never believe who just walked into this Dinner. Little Elizabeth Cole, Beth's granddaughter. My god she looks like death warmed over. She has just let herself go, it's no wonder her husband left her." Listen that is the short version of the phone call. She would of course go into more details about just how pathetic I looked.

By the time the last call is made the story would sound something like, " Did you hear Elizabeth is back in town. Her husband and her are getting divorce because she caught him in bed with another man. Of course with the way she has let herself go I can't blame him for changing teams. A drunk, blind, bum wouldn't even put his dick in her." Like I said whisper down the lane.

So since, I refuse to give the gossip mill at least a weeks worth of material I was going to have to go without food, or caffeine. In fact, if I hadn't grabbed my toiletries bag and a change of clothes out of the truck last night I wouldn't be taking a shower until after it got dark tonight. The gossip spies have probably been pacing up and down the street with binoculars, like a pack of staving vultures since I pulled in last night. I climbed the stairs to the second floor. Holding my breath as I opened my bedroom door. I have no idea what color paint home decorating senior Barbie picked out. I was actually pleasantly surprised. Nana had found the perfect color. It was a light lilac with just a tiny bit of dove grey mixed in. The two shades combined to create the palest grey purple I had ever seen. Her phenomenal color choice for my bedroom did not change how much I hated what she wanted to do in my office.

Which was something I needed to talk to Brandon about. I slammed my head into the wall next to my shower. I had forgotten all about Brandon coming over. With my luck, he would be standing on my front steps in the next five minutes. Screw him. He could wait, I needed this shower more than I needed my floor done. Besides I was almost one hundred and ten percent sure Nan had made sure to give him a key.

I stood under the hot water, letting it run down my shoulders and back. The scalding water, quickly turned my pale skin bright pink. I stood under the water head down, leaning against the wall for longer than I had planned. I shut the water off as it turned cold, feeling like a new woman. Every surface of my body had been, shave, scrubbed, buffed, and polished. There were no traces of the last month left on my skin.

" Pige, now that the hot water tank is empty, I brought you a cup of coffee. I'll see you in the kitchen. " He yelled thru the door. I cocked my head to the side trying to figure out how the hell he had gotten in the house. Nana, the dirty rotten women had clearly given him a key. Damn it. I quickly threw on my favorite jeans. They sat low on my hips and hugged my ass like a second skin. My breasts protested as I confined them in a bra for the first time in a month. I quickly threw on my black tank top and walked towards the smell of coffee. My hair hung damp down my back, and I still had no makeup on. But I was clean. That was as big of a step back into the world of the living as I would be taking today.

" Hey," I held up my hand as I entered the kitchen, in some pathetic wave.

" Oh my god, Pigeon you actually look alive this morning. I don't know what kind of water you are pumping in here, but it can perform miracles." He said. I punched him in the shoulder on my way to the coffee.

" Thanks for this." I held the coffee up in his general direction, before taking a large swig.

" After last night, I figured you might need it." He laughed as the cup stopped at my lips. I could feel my eyes growing wide, and

I panicked over what happened last night. For the life of me, me I couldn't remember.

"Oh god," I could feel the blush creeping up my neck. "What happened?" I stared at my feet, suddenly terrified to make eye contact with him. Which seems ridiculous. For the love of god this man took my virginity. He stood leaning against the doorframe, one foot crossed over the other. I have no idea if I had gotten drunk last night. But I was clearly drunk right now because Brandon was looking down right sexy. I am going chalk it up to not normally seeing a man standing in my kitchen in a pair of jean. That and I clearly am, not in possession of a stable mind.

" Don't worry girl, there's no need to blush. You didn't do anything other than cry, and get drunk off of two beers." He said his eyes danced in the morning light. " That and mumbled some crazy nonsense about hating the color of your office while I carried you into the house."

The coffee flew out of my mouth. " I let you carry me into the house? I was that bad from two beers?" I was silently wishing for a sinkhole to magically appear under my feet right now.

" Well you fought me at first, with some bull shit that sounded like 'No don't touch me, I smelly, you can't get to close I'll contaminate your sex with my stink.' But I carried you in anyway. Mostly because you flipped yourself out of the hammock, and fell in a bush as you attempted to stand up." He said attempting to muffle his laughter. " Thank god you showered, wouldn't want to be contaminated." He was no longer trying to hide is laughter, as he is face broke out in a wide grin.

I shrugged my shoulders. " What can I say I hadn't really eaten in days, and you already knew I was a light weight." I am silently praying he lets the drunken comments go. I did not need to explain that I had actually called him sexy last night.

" You can tell yourself that if you need to Pige." He winked at me, taking another sip of his coffee. " So about the office, now that you are sober. I know what Nan wants. But this is your house. Come on up stairs and tell me how you want the office to look, and what you need to be at your creative best." He turned and walked out of the kitchen. Not bothering to see if I was following. Which I wasn't. Currently I am standing with my jaw on the floor. Brandon was making it exceedingly hard to hate him. First the jeans that made his ass look like a Greek god. Plus I honestly think he is the first person to ever consider or care about for that matter what I need to let my creativity shine. In fact, I don't think my husband ever stopped to consider that even for a half of a millisecond.

" Pige, you coming or what? You've got thirty seconds, or I'm painting it the color Nan wanted." Brandon's voice echoed against the empty walls. I set my coffee down and sprinted up the stairs taking them two at a time.

" Sorry, I was just trying to figure out exactly what I want my office to look like." I said trying to catch my breath.

" Wait, wait wait, you don't have any idea what you want your office to look like?" His nose scrunched up in confusion. I shook my head no. "Really, I thought you would have had some idea, there is nothing you want to carry over from your office in Boston?"

" No, to all of the above." I shrugging my shoulders I sat down in the middle of the floor. Trying to picture what I seriously wanted my office to look like.

" Let me guess, this is going to be just like your bedroom in Boston correct. That controlling no dick prick vetoed it didn't he?" Brandon stood in front of me, hands on his hips, with hints of fury creeping into his eyes. I just nodded my head yes. There undoubtedly was nothing else to say to that. Brandon sank down next to me, silently waiting for me to decide the fate of the walls.

Mandelyn Kilroy

" Hey Bran, do you think we could paint the only wall in the room that doesn't have any windows or doors a deep hot pink, the rest of the walls white, and maybe all the wood work and doors black?" The door to enter the room sat in the middle of one wall. Once you walked in the door to the right is closet, which broke up that wall. To the left were two windows breaking up another wall. Leaving the wall I wanted to be an accent, and remarkably bold.

" If that's what you want then that's what I will do. I think it will look amazing. I have an idea that you may like as well. Hear me out." He held his hand up to silence my complaint. I will do everything that you want. But how would you feel about the other three walls with very large white stripes, with tiny hot pink and black pinstripes breaking them up?" I closed my eyes letting the image sink into my brain.

" I love it. Brandon thank you for asking what I needed in here." I nudged my knee into his.

" Your welcome Pige. Just don't tell Nan it was my idea to change what she wanted. Okay? I kind of enjoy my head attached to my neck." His knee bumped into mine.

" Where the hell did the nick name Pigeon come from?" I laughed. For as long as I can remember he has called me Pigeon, or Pige for short, and I had no idea why.

" Darling, that's a secret I'm going to keep." He said as he rose up from the floor. Turning to offer me his hand. I rolled my eyes as I let him pull me to my feet.

" Sooner or later I am going to get it out of you." I said as I walked out of the room. For the first time in a while, I had the tiniest pep in my step.

CHAPTER SIX
Elizabeth

The pep in my step was short lived. By noon, Madison and my grandmother were standing in my back yard. My laptop had been forcefully removed from my lap, and they were three seconds away from physically dragging me off the property.

" Guy can we please do this another day?" I had spent the last fifteen minutes refusing to participate in their newest half-baked plan. I was debating about tying myself to the tree. Not that it would stop them.

" No, we can not. Now get up all three of us have appointments, and they are not easy to get." Madison's hands hit her hips, and I knew she meant business. She was now using her full on mom voice.

" Aw Pige stop being a party pooper and go. She's actually really good. Besides it will be fun." Brandon said from the kitchen door.

" You too, seriously? Out of everyone I thought that you would be on my side in regards to visiting a psychic." I threw a desperate glance in his direction. Begging him silently to save me.

" Not me Pige, I have seen her a few times. I will be fun.

From here to forever

Something I think you could use, because clearly you have not had fun in your life in a long time." He sauntered towards me.

" Don't you dare Brandon. I was drunk last night and couldn't fight with you to put me down." I screamed as he threw me over his shoulder.

" Who's car am I child locking her in?" He laughed as he carried me thru the house.

" Brandon, I just want you to be well aware that when you least expect it I am going to punch you in the fucking face." I hissed, only making him laugh harder.

" Yeah, yeah, yeah, I'm shaking in my boots. If I put you down will you please play along for the two of them? They are both really worried about you?" I let out a heavy sigh.

" Yeah I'll behave." I felt my feet hit the pavement, but his hands stayed firm on my waist.

" I'm serious Pige, you need this more than you know." His eyes bore into mine, with an unfamiliar intensity.

" I know you are Bran, I cross my heart. I will try to have fun." I whispered, suddenly unable to raise my voice any louder. His hands were still on my waist keeping me just a few inches from his body.

" You ready to go?" Nan's voice broke thru the haze that had settled around us. Brandon's hands quickly fell away from my waist.

" She's good to go Nan." Brandon leaned over and quickly kissed her check. " She was just telling me how she is actually a little curious about Lillian, and thinks it maybe a lot of fun." He coyly smiled over Nan's head, winking at me as Nan grabbed my arm.

" Oh good darling, because you are going first. Come on now lets get in the car Madison will be right out. She was just grabbing your purse." Brandon stepped around her, opening her door.

Offering his hand to Nan as she climbed in. His hip rested against my door, preventing me from getting in the car. He shut her door stepping back to reach for my door handle while still blocking me from getting in the car.

" Remember you promised to at least fake fun darling." He said so quiet that only I could hear.

" I don't normally fake it, but I will put on a happy face and play nice in the sand box." I said as he stepped out of my way. I slide into the backseat, looking up at Brandon and smiling my best pretend smile.

He leaned into the car ever so slightly. " Hey Pige there is no way in hell you can honestly tell me you didn't spend every night of your marriage faking it." With that, he shut the door before I could formulate a response. I rolled my eyes and turned towards the front of the car. Only to find two sets of shoulders shaking with laughter.

" Okay ladies, let go see your psychic. How much did you tell her about me?" I said I would put on a good show for them, and trust me if it means I can get the two of them off of my back I am going to give them one hell of a performance. But I never said I wouldn't be skeptical. Just like I wouldn't put it past the two of them to tell her what they wanted me to hear.

" Seriously Iz, have a little faith in us. " I caught my best friend rolling her eyes in the rearview mirror.

" Hey, I was just asking ok. I don't know how these things work." I threw my hands up. There was no way I was going convince them I was having fun if I started a fight five minutes into our trip.

" It's fine. Just try to have an open mind okay?" I nodded my head in agreement before turning to stare out the window. I was rolling my eyes as we turned into the psychics drive way. If this woman was anything like her yard, she was a looney toon. The

From here to forever

massive oak that sat in the middle of her yard was painted. Yes, you read that right I said the tree was painted. I'm not talking a few spots of paint on the tree. I'm talking a rainbow of rings around the tree trunk painted at least fourteen feet up the tree. Yeah I'm sure this could be cute if we were living in wonderland, and it was only a few colors. But we are not in wonderland, and there are easily two hundred different colored rings around this tree. If it were only the tree that was out of this world, I would calk it up to a drunken idea. However below the tree there stood at least two hundred gnomes, all posed to look like they were living in a little town. I am not even exaggerating when I say this. There were ten of them lying in hammocks. I climbed out of the car, trying to avoid taking in any more of the yard. I was terrified of what I would find, the gnomes and the tree have me a little concerned we are about to enter an extremely insane woman's home.

" My little roses, how lovely to see you." A high-pitched nasal voice caused me to look up. If I had thought her yard was insane, I had no words to describe her appearance. In fact, I think it was making the yard look normal. Lillian had to be easily sixty-five. She had hot pink, purple, and blue hair down to her butt. The only way to describe her outfit is starting at her feet, and working my way up. It will help prevent your brain from exploding.

On her feet were fuzzy frog slippers in a puke green hue. She had on leopard leggings, with a variety of rainbow scarves tied around her waist. Which I am assuming is supposed to be a skirt. Instead, it looked like she has gotten tangles in the clothes line, and had not bothered to re-hang up the wash. Here is where your head may still explode. I just want to brace you, brains on a book is never a good look. She didn't have a shirt on. Yes, you read that right. I am currently staring at a sixty five year old woman who is wearing only a see thru lace bra as her top. Sadly I can also tell you that she has both of her nipples pierced and her belly button. If you just threw up in your mouth, you are not alone, I just swallowed mine. She stepped towards me, and I quickly masked my horror. As I said before I think she is mentally unstable, a few crayon short of a full box, adding two and two together and getting fifty-seven, whatever you want to call it. The last thing I want to do is to offend her. That's how you end up tied up in a basement being force feed chicken food.

"Doll, your life is in turmoil, and full of great pain and confusion." She took my hand and led me into her house. " I will start with her, you two there is food in the kitchen." She waved her hand towards the back of the house, before leading me into a small room just inside the door. " Sit my darling girl, lets begin and see if there is any hope of calm in your future." I watched her shuffle the cards that sat on the table. I didn't say anything to her, not even hello. No, I was not being a bitch. I just remembered hearing once you shouldn't say to much when you get your cards read. The less you give them the faster you can figure out if they are a fake. Not that I believe in this kind of crap. She slides the cards towards me.

" Please shuffle then set the deck back down and cut it into three piles to the left." Her voice was like nails on a chalkboard, it was grinding on my already frayed nerves. I did as she asked making sure to close my eyes when I cut the pile three times to the left. I don't know why I closed my eyes, so don't bother asking. You close you eyes when you kiss and when you wish, so I figure if I am going to mess with fate might as well close my eyes. I sat back waiting to see how she was going twist what she had already been told about me. She lay the cards in front of my in an intricate design.

" As I said when you came in you are suffering from great heartache. The cards see it, and you aura is damaged from it. This card here is the queen of swords she represents new life. But here she revealed herself upside down, which means you could not or did not want a new life." She paused raising and eyebrow at me. I gave her nothing, no nod, no verbal clues. I just sat staring at the cards. " Ah how fascinating here you have not one but two knights." She sat staring at the cards, rubbing her chin. The suspense was killing me.

" Why is it fascinating Lillian?"

" You see this one here?" She tapped the card to the left of the queen. " This knight is also upside down. You and you husband are separated and or divorced? Recently in-fact. That is not what is so fascinating, you think he left because of the queen, and you are very wrong." She paused again staring at the cards. I seriously do not understand how cards can tell her so damn much. I mean really, in a game a solitaire if you flip the ace of clubs over, and it's upside down it still means the exact same thing.

" Then why did he leave me?" My voice sounded much more annoyed than I currently intended it to sound.

" You are not going to like the answer to that." She said as she flipped out more cards in front of her. " Well that is very very peculiar." She paused yet again. This woman was killing me. She is like the reality show contest result show, with a commercial break every sixty second.

" What, what is so peculiar?" I no longer cared if I sounded annoyed. Lillian was dangling answers in front of me. Answers to questions I have spent the last month asking myself.

" The cards are saying work, or another woman." I sat staring at her, extremely disappointed in myself. How could I have actually believed that any of this was real? Women, or work, those were two of the main reasons behind most divorces. That really wasn't a far stretch. To make this entire situation worse. I was done playing this card game, and I couldn't even walk away. Not because I was still interested. No, no because I wanted to get everyone off of my ass and that was not going to happen unless I made them think I was having fun. Walking out of my reading before it was over was only going to plant Tweedle Dee and Tweedle Dumb even father up my ass.

" So you said the two knights were fascinating right? So what about the other knight?" I smiled at her tapping the poor forgotten knight.

" Oh yes, it is very peculiar that you got both of these knights on either side of the queen. While the last knight signifies a lost love. This knight signifies a lost love returning." I held up my hand cutting her off before she could finish.

" Okay Lillian, out with it. How much did they tell you about me and my current situation?" I was now standing in front of her taping my foot.

" Nothing, they did not even tell me your name. When Madison called all she said was the two of them needed to make an appointment, and she wanted to bring a friend who was a non-believer. I swear darling, I am not pulling your leg. Besides if I was do you honestly think I'd tell you that the first person to break your heart is back in your life, and that the person to fix that broken heart left you for work or another woman. Get the hell out of here, if I had known all of that before you walked in here Id' tell you that you were going to come into money, and have great sex, and move the hell on from these two." She held the knight cards up in my face. I slowly sat back down.

" I'm sorry, it's just I felt like this was a terribly cruel joke." I sheepishly smiled at her. Lillian reached over and patted my arm.

" I understand. Would you like to continue?" She held the deck up in front of me. I nodded my head. Watching as more cards hit the table. " Well, darling I honestly don't have much you will find good at this junction in your life. Your love life is going to remain

From here to forever

full of complicated feelings for a while. However it does not appear that your heart is complicated. It's your head that is complicating these feelings. Once you allow your heart to lead you will find the answers you have been looking for. Only when your head can accept the answers will your heart lead. Are you a writer?" She looked up at me waiting for a response. I was still trying to understand her last statement.

" Yes, yes I am a writer." I answered.

" This card represents your creativity and muse. The universe is providing you with many story lines. You are just to close to them to really appreciate them at this time. Soon enough you will look back and understand all of the hurt." She lay the rest of the cards down. " Did you have any questions for me?" she asked.

" Yes I do, when do we get to the great sex you were talking about earlier. Is any of that in my future?" I teased.

" Doll, you must find out about yourself before you can find each other. Only then will the great sex come." She stood up taking my hands in hers. " But when the great sex and the great love comes you make sure to invite me to the wedding." She leaned down and kissed my check before leaving the room. I sat staring at all of the cards that lay spread out before me. So maybe she was a psychic, but this was not fun. Everything she told me was well lets be honest, either depressing, cryptic, or very unclear. I probably should go find Madison and Nan, so they can see that I went thru with the entire reading, and possibly had fun. No, I can't honestly call it fun, it was mind boggling, and I now have plenty to mull over tonight when I am not sleeping.

" There you are. So did you have fun, what did she tell you?" Nan jumped up off of the bar stool when I walked into the kitchen.

" Aren't you guys getting reading?" I asked. I did not want to spend all day here and both of them were still sitting here staring at me.

" No, that was a little white lie to get you to agree to come. Nan and I had readings done a little over a month ago, so we are both good. Now out with it what did she tell you?" Madison looped her arm thru mine and started towards the front door. Nan fell into step on my other side. I just want you to be aware I am pissed. These bitched not only lied to me, but also lead me here under false pretenses. They were about to get a taste of their own medicine.

" She told me that I am going to be better of without Jonathan. But it is going to take me a little bit of time to get over him. While I am trying to get over him, I am going to have a lot of sex, with multiple people. She said that is how I am going to get rid of my anger towards him, and that it will help me feel confident again." I slide into the back seat of the car not even feeling bad. " She also said the I'm going to have a very hot sex induced fling with someone from my past." I watched both of their faces pale. I turned and stared out of the window, attempting to hold back my laughter. There was not a word uttered in the car until we turned onto my street.

" Listen guys, I was just joking. She didn't say any of that. I'm not really sure I understand what she told me. Can I wrap my head around, and then I will share it with you?" They both turned looking at me as the car came to a stop in my driveway.

"Of course." They said in unison.

" Thank you, and thanks for today I actually had a good time. It was very interesting, and a little unnerving." I laughed pulling them both into a tight hug. I climbed out of the car watching Madison back down the driveway. She was a good friend, not many people would insist on driving around the block to drop Nan off. Especially when it actually take Nan less time took less to cut thru our back yards. I waved as they drove away. When I turned around Brandon was leaning against the front door.

" So did you actually have fun, or was that all an act?" He asked.

" I wouldn't say I had fun. But that wasn't fake just now. They are both happy with me, and a little less worried." I sighed at the disappointment that still found its way into his expression.

" So if you didn't have fun, how did you pull off getting them to be less worried?" Brandon was starting to panic. He had always been the master at wrapping Nan around his finger. I could see the doubt in his abilities creeping across his face.

" I had a very long reading, I didn't walk out of it till it was over. I told them that I needed to mull over everything she had told me in order to sort it all out and wrap my head around it all before I can explain what she told me. That seemed to satisfy them. I just can't describe what I just did as fun. It was more nerve wreaking and confusing than fun." I shrugged my shoulders as I pushed past him.

" Hey Pige, if it's any consolation you look like you had fun." He reached into his pocket lighting a cigarette as I closed the front door. I quietly walked thru my house, picking up my computer and heading for the back yard. I was going to spend some time researching those damn cards.

CHAPTER SEVEN
Brandon

I knew damn right well that I had been seriously pushing her buttons earlier. But it needed to be done. If her grandmother and Madison hadn't figured out the art of pushing her buttons yet, then I was going to have to step up to the plate. Pige never wants to be wrong so she will do anything she can to be right. Even if it means she is going to have a terrible time doing it. I should feel ashamed for manipulating her, but she needed to get out of the house and try to have some fun. Sitting around staring at a blank computer screen, was only going to let her wallow in her own self-pity. Pige had this terrible habit of living inside of her own head. So the longer she was permitted to sit staring into the abyss the harder it was going to be for her to snap out of this depression.

Okay that and Nan had drug me to see Lillian three weeks ago, and I wanted to know if Pige was told anything like what I had been told. My reading had been forty-five minutes long, and the only thing I remember being told was a past relationship that hadn't been given a proper chance was going to get a second chance. I spent the rest of my reading trying to figure out whom the second chance was going to be with. Never in a million years did I even stop to consider, it would have been the girl I once planned on making my wife. Before she opened the front door a little over twenty-four hours ago, I did my best not to ever think about her. It didn't hurt as much that way. Of course, I knew if I sat down with a shrink I would be told the reason I jump from girl to girl, ending every relationship before things get to serious is because I am still holding a torch for Pige.

Pige brushed by me on her way into the house. From the look on her face, she did not want to talk about what had happened. In fact, she looked like she wanted to kill all three of us for making her go. She would get over it sooner or later, she always did. She was however going to kill me in about three minutes since I had just told her some seriously distressing news about her house. I snubbed out my cigarette as I braced myself for her freak-out. I walked thru the house looking for her. Her computer was no longer sitting on her mattress, which means more than likely she was sitting out back staring at a blank screen. I stood at the kitchen door searching for her. The gate in the corner of her yard was open, and she was gone.

" Damn it." I yelled. I needed to get her okay before I could continue working. Until I found her this project was at a stand still. I knew she couldn't have gotten far. But I was mildly concerned.

I don't know if you have noticed, but Pige hasn't exactly been mentally in touch with the real world as of late. Which means she could end up in some crazy situation without even realizing it until she was in serious trouble. I sighed as I walked across the back yard. Stopping at the gate looking up and down the street in either direction. Of course, she was nowhere in sight.

" Perfect this is just perfect. Leave it to Pige to make my life more difficult then it has to be. God this woman drives me crazy. She is single handedly going to send me on a vacation to a quiet padded cell.

From here to forever

Four hours later I had visited every shop in town. Only to discover no one had seen her, and half of them had no idea she was even back in town. I sat in my truck trying to figure out where she could be. Truthfully, I'm actually starting to get very worried that she is laying dead in a ditch somewhere. The sun was setting, and I certainly didn't want her wandering around in the dark if she wasn't in that ditch. I couldn't help but notice how the brilliant sunset made the water tower look whiter then it truly was. I threw the car in drive. I hadn't been to the water tower since the night before she left. But if there was one place either of us would run to when we needed to think, and sort out our lives it would be the water tower.

I said a silent prayer that she was there. I sent Candice a text that we had to push dinner back a few hours because of a work emergency, and then I raced down the dirt trail. Getting as close as I could to the small path that lead to what had once been our own secret meeting place. I was sprinting down the trail without even meaning to. I can't explain why I am so worried about that girl. She is after all a grown up and has been taking care of herself for years. But I was secretly terrified something terrible was going to happen to rip her out of my life again, and possible for good this time.

I hunched over as I reached the clearing trying to catch my breath. My eyes searched the top of the tower in the dim light of dusk. I could barely make her out. But there she was sitting in the exact spot I had found her in thousands of times growing up. I couldn't help but smile. She was going thru hell, and I was over joyed at finally having a reason to visit the place that had seen so many life changing moments in my life. I took a step forward, my breath hitched in my chest as I tried to decided if I could actually bring myself to climb up there. I didn't want to run the risk that the magic that always seemed to float thru the air at the top no

Mandelyn Kilroy

longer being there. Then again I don't know if I can handle sitting down next to her with that very magic wrapping around us like a cocoon. I leaned my head against the ladder taking a deep breath trying to calm my heart. There was only one way to find out if the magic still existed. I placed my foot on the ladder said a silent prayer as I pulled myself up.

CHAPTER EIGHT
Elizabeth

I have been sitting on top of this damn water tower for the last three hours. I'm not quite sure how I ended up here. In fact the last time I was up here was the night before I left for college. It had once been my sanctuary. The place I ran to when I need to think, or cry, or secretly meet Brandon. Most of the time it was when I was secretly meeting Brandon. This water tower knows all of my darkest secrets. The day my mother walked back into my life thirteen years after giving birth to me, only to sign her parental rights over to Nan. This exact spot is where I ran. It also watched as Brandon and I crossed the line from friendship to grey area to planning forever. I traced the B and the P that had been carved into the railing the last time we had been up here. I can't help but smile, as I remember the fight we had had over him carving a P instead of an E. It seems like silly a thing to fight over now, but at the time it had been the most important thing in the world.

" But Pige, I do not ever call you anything other than Pige. Putting a god damn E next to the B would cause this to lose some serious sentimental meaning." He had yelled, slamming his fists down on the railing.

From here to forever

" Bran, I want the E because no one will know that this carving is about me and you." I screamed back stomping my feet in frustration. Brandon had stormed toward me, cupping my face in his hands.

" Pige this isn't about everybody else. This is about right here, and right now. It's about my feelings for you. This is about you and me forever. You and me Pige." I had thrown myself at him. My lips crushing against his, as my leg hitched around his waist. He pulled back to soon. I could have spent hours kissing him. But neither one of us had wanted that night to end. It was the last night of our childhood in so many ways, and we didn't want to waste it with our eyes closed, and lips locked. I had sat with my legs wrapped around his waist, and my breast pressed into his back, holding him tightly to me, as he carved B+P=4ever into the railing. Before we climbed down that night, I had pressed my lips to the carving, silently wishing that there could be a forever. I already knew there was never going to be. The next day I would be leaving for college, and everything would be changing.

I quickly shook my head, wiping away the stray tears that had slipped past my lashes. That memory always caused me to cry . For the last ten years it has been the memory that reminded me just how beautiful first loves can be, and just how heart wrenching it is when they are over.

" Thought I'd find you here." Brandon whispered as he slides down next to me.

" Yeah well, I needed to clear my head, and this has always been the place I ran to." I shrugged my shoulders.

" Listen Pige about earlier." Brandon started. I held my hand up to silence him.

" Brandon please, I can take anymore today okay?" I let my head fall against the railing.

" God damn it Elizabeth will you just listen to me." His hands slammed into the railing, vibrating my head. I pulled back and stared at him. I could list the number of times he had called me anything other than Pige or Pigeon on one hand. " I get it okay, I do. You didn't want to move back here. Once you got here your grandmother took over and created some huge project and now you have to deal with the mess. The mess that I helped creates tonight. I get it okay. Your upset and nothing is going your way right now. But damn it some bad news about the floor shouldn't have set you off like that. At least it wouldn't have set off the girl I know, or well knew." He fell silent next to me. I let my head fall once more into the railing. He was right, what had happened earlier was not me but it had been the breaking point. He was right it wasn't his fault at all. In fact it was my fault for not realizing there was a serious problem with the floor when I purchased the house. I was trying desperately not to re-live the freak out that had unfolded hours ago. It was unavoidable, I was just going to give in to the memory, maybe then I would have a better idea of how to apologize.

" Listen Pige, I have some bad news. " Brandon stood in the backyard hands shoved in his pockets. He had spent most of the day pulling up the carpets in the second floor. His original plan of doing one room at a time had gone right out the window, after we discovered it would be significantly cheaper to rent a dumpster for the old carpet for a day or two. Rather than pay to have the carpet hauled away after each room. I shut my computer, in order to give him my full attention, and to ignore the blank page I had been staring at for hours. My creativity seemed to have stayed in Boston with my heart.

" What kind of problem Brandon?" I was starting to panic at the seriousness in his voice.

" So I got all of the carpet pulled up on the second floor. Were you informed that there was the possibility of water damage when you purchased the house?" He sat down across me at the patio table.

" No, no one said a word about water damage. Why, what's wrong?" I could hear the panic in my voice, and I fought against the urge to rush inside.

" Well under the carpet are hardwood floors. Which are ruined, beyond repair. In fact they are so warped, and weak I honestly think it is unsafe to even attempt to salvage any part of them. Pige it looks like water sat on those floors for a while, and rather than fix it carpet was just put down to hide it." He said, waiting for me to respond.

" So you have to remove all of the floors?" I was holding my breath terrified of what his answer would be.

" Yeah Pige, I have to remove the floor, and the ceiling for the first floor." I started to interrupt him, but he held his hand up silencing me. " I pulled up one board and the support beams were damaged by the water, or the weight of the water sitting on the floor. I'm going to have to replace the support beams as well." I slammed my hands down on the table.

" Of course, of fucking course you do. Why wouldn't that need to be done? I mean seriously it's not like any part of me even wanted this stupid house re-done. Hell, I never wanted to live in it. I only bought it to shut up my grandmother. You know what the common trend has been in my life recently? Everybody else continues to tell me what they want. Which always effects me, and in the end they get what they want and I get screwed." I screamed at him before I stormed out of the backyard, thru the house, and left on foot. I didn't want to be followed, or found.

I opened my eyes, and looked over at Brandon. " I'm really sorry about earlier Bran. I was really out of line. You see the thing is my home was broken long before you pulled the carpet up today. I am just so done trying to rebuild it. I just don't have the energy to put into attempting to rebuild something that clearly should just stay broken." A tear trickled down my check. For the second night in a row, I was crying in front of Brandon. I expected him to say something to comfort me. I felt his hand on my check. I turned my head so my check was resting in his hand. My eyes were closed but I could feel him lean closer to me. My eyes flew open as his lips pressed into mine. I should push him away from me, stop this. But the feeling of another pair of lips on mine was almost comforting. For a moment I let my self get lost in the familiarity of kissing on this water tower. For just a moment I was eighteen again, and my heart wasn't broken. I slide my hand up to the back of his neck as he started to pull away. His forehead resting against mine.

" Sorry, if that was out of line. I just couldn't handle watching you cry again, it almost killed me last night." He whispered.

" Bran I really am sorry, I shouldn't keep taking everything out on you." I whispered back.

" Darling, you can take it out on me any time you want. But I think maybe you should start talking about what really going on in that pretty little head of yours." He said as he pulled back standing up. He held out his hand to me waiting to help me up.

" I think I'm going to sit here a little longer Bran. I'll be okay, and thanks for everything." I smiled up at him, trying to reassure him I actually was okay.

" Your right Pige you will be okay." He replied as he started down the ladder. I sat quietly watching him walk away from the water tower, his head down, hands in his pockets as the last of the sun set disappeared beyond the horizon in front of him. Maybe he is right, maybe it's time I started talking about what had happened, and how I was dealing with it. I couldn't move on if I continued to hold onto the past. But was Brandon part of that past, and did I genuinely want to let him go? I honestly think I just need to live on an island all by myself until I figure out what I want in life. It would be so much easier that way.

" I'm so confused," I needed to say it out loud, and there was no one around to hear me except the water tower. That statement was a tiny bloop on the Richter scale of secrets I have shared with the water tower. It has been witness so so many monumental moments and first in my life. This was the exact spot I opened my college acceptance letter at, where I said good-bye to my hometown before I left, and the place I first kissed Brandon when we were fourteen. It was actually kind of ironic, the water tower is the only thing in the world that has any idea what actually has happened between Brandon and I. I climbed to my feet, finally ready to go home.

" Good night my old friend. Thank you for always being here." I said quietly before I climbed back down the ladder. I quietly started down the trail that leads to Main Street, lost in thought.

" You know I haven't been back up there since the night you left." I couldn't help but jump at the sound of his voice.

" I thought you had gone home." I clutched my chest, waiting for my heart to regain normal beating.

" I never said I was going home. I just left to give you the time you needed." He fell into step beside me.

" You really never went back?" I was shocked by his omissions.

" No, it never felt right without you. In fact it actually kind of felt right not to go back. That was the place I first kissed you, and were I thought I had said good bye to you forever." I sighed.

" You do know I never wanted to say good bye to you forever right?" I stopped reaching for his arm to stop him. He nodded his head yes, before we continued on our walk in silence.

" Pige, I just want you to know if you decide your ready to talk about what happened up in Boston, I will always be here to listen." He finally broke the silence, as we reached my front door.

" I know thanks." I leaned forward and pressed my lips to his check.

"Pige you do know that it isn't exactly safe to sleep in there correct." He reached out and stopped my hand from turning the door nob.

" Why not." I tried to hide the disappointment from my voice.

" Pige you are missing a ceiling in half of the down stairs, and your second floor support beams are damaged. I just don't feel safe letting you sleep here tonight." He pulled my hand away from the door, trapping it within his own.

" So where am I supposed to stay." The last thing I wanted was to sleep at my grandmothers for the next few days.

" I grabbed you shower bag and lap top they are in my truck, you can stay with me if you want." He squeezed my hand. " I have a guest room that is. Please don't think I was suggesting anything else." I couldn't help but laugh as he tried to back track.

" Bran a towel on the kitchen floor would be perfectly fine, as long as I am not at Nan's I'll be a happy girl. You guest bedroom or couch will be perfect. Are you sure I'm not putting you out?" I held my breath. For some strange reason the only place I wanted to be was at his house.

" Not at all cookie." He led me to his truck, once again opening my door for me. There on the floor by my feet sat my computer bag, toiletries bag, and my nightshirt and short that had been handing on the bathroom door.

" Thanks, I really appreciate it." I smiled as he backed down my driveway.

" Listen Pige once I get you all settled in, I have to go out for a bit. I kind of blew someone off last night, and I have to make it up to her tonight." I could feel his eyes on me, but I was frozen. That news had been a giant kick in the gut. He was just kissing me not even an hour ago, and now he was rushing off to his girlfriend. I mean clearly I had been stupid not to assume he had a girlfriend.

" Brand I'm so sorry I did not mean to mess up a date last night." I was fighting to hide my disappointment.

" Don't worry she understood, and you won't be completely alone. Maggie my lab will keep you company." He said as he turned up a driveway. " Well this is it."

" Your parents place?" I smiled as I sat staring at the brick cape cod where I had been a part of so many family dinners. Only to climb up the lattice outside of Brandon's bedroom window after his parents had gone to bed.

" Yeah well you know dad died four years ago. After that mom packed up and moved to Florida to live with her sister who was widowed as well. So I bought the house and took over the business." He shrugged his shoulders. I had comeback to town when his father died. Not that Brandon and I had a chance to speak other then when I offered my condolences at the funeral. I had been in the middle of a book tour when my grandmother called me with the news. In order to be at the service I had taken a red eye the night before from San Francisco and had to immediately fly back to LA the same day. In fact I had literally been in town for less then six hours that day. But I needed to say goodbye to his father. He had been such a vital part of my life for so long. I never would have been able to live with myself if I hadn't made it. My public relations rep was not happy with my decision, but agreed to it as long as I was back in LA by four am the next day to do the morning talk show I was booked on.

"Are you going to make me climb the lattice to get in, or can I use the front door." I teased as I climbed out of the car.

" Darlin if you want to climb the lattice more power to you, but you can use the front door." He opened the door. Blocking my body with his. I took a step back as the thunder of paws echoed down the dark hallway. Before I could brace myself a giant ball of chocolate fur hurled herself at me, knocking me to the ground and covering me with warm wet dog kisses. " Off Maggie." The kisses quickly stopped. When I opened my eyes I discovered that Brandon was holding her back, so I could get to my feet. " Sorry about that Pige."

" Don't worry. Who doesn't want a greeting like that?" I laughed as I rubbed the top of her head. Brandon released her keeping his hand on her collar. Maggie instantly glued herself to my side.

" Looks like you have a new best friend. She doesn't normally take to strangers like that." He couldn't hide the shock in his voice, as he watched how Maggie danced around me begging for attention.

" Guess I'm lucky." I teased as I walked into the house.

" Listen Pige, I really have to go. There is food in the fridge, and the guest room is my old bedroom. You know where everything else is make your self at home." He was starting back out the door.

" Have fun Bran, I'll see you later." I waved as he closed the door. I waited until I heard his truck back down the driveway before I sank to the floor, pulling out my cell phone.

" Hey, are you ready to tell me what your future holds?" Madison chirped into the phone before it had rang more then once.

" Why didn't you tell me he had a girlfriend?" Screw Madison and her need to know what my future held. She had with held information I needed to know. She could just keep waiting for the answerers she wanted.

" Who Brandon? Why would that matter Iz?" She shot back. " Oh my god you are still in love with him aren't you?"

" No I hate him, I will always hate him. Especially after what he did earlier tonight. I mean seriously how dare he kiss me on top of the water tower, invite me to stay at his house because mine is uninhabitable at the moment, tell me I can sleep in his old room once we get here, and then drop me off at the door and rush off to go pick up some dizzy bitch." I had no intention of sounding like a pissed off five year old. Regardless that is exactly what I sounded like.

" He's been seeing some girl from the next town over for a few months. It's nothing serious, it never is. Did you say he kissed you, and you are sitting in his house alone right now?"

" Madison keep up. Yes he kissed me on top of the water tower earlier." I sighed

" The same water tower were you lost your virginity to him?" She asked, a little to excited. If I could slap her through the phone I would right now.

" Yup in the exact spot where he took my virginity, and I'm not alone in his house. Maggie his dog is here with me." I said, as I reached down and ran my fingers threw Maggie's fur. Her head was resting in my lap content now that she was touching me. I was desperate trying not to be pissed at Madison for not telling me about Brandon's girlfriend, and for bringing up the complete history of the water tower.

" So how long are you staying with him?" Her voice was so filled with excitement; I am sure by now she is standing in her kitchen with a glass of wine, eating popcorn, and basking in the excitement of my life.

" I am only staying tonight. Tomorrow I am going to stay at Nan's or my own house. I seriously shouldn't be here now. It's not fair to take advantage of someone I hate so god damn much. " I hissed. " And my life is not your own personal soap opera, so stop getting so much enjoyment out of tragedy I am living in.

" Iz, have you ever stopped to think, maybe the reason you hate him so much is because you are still very much in love with him?" I could hear her holding her breath on the other end of the line.

Mandelyn Kilroy

" I'm not in love with him." I screamed into the phone, right before I threw it across the room. " Come on Maggie lets go to bed. I climbed the stairs to the guest bedroom. The house looked nothing like when his parents had owned it. When we were growing up the stair well was covered in candid family shots, and the walls were all painted warm golds, browns, and reds. Now the stair well was empty, and the warm walls had been replaced with a light cream, and dove grey. I ran my hand up the hand carved cherry banister, his mother spent hours wrapping fresh pine garland around each Christmas. I was actually have a difficult time accepting just how much a place I had considered a second home growing up had changed. I walked down the hall at the top of the stairs. I didn't need to a light I could find his room in my sleep. I paused outside of his childhood bedroom. I wasn't ready to face the thought that room being changed. I took a deep breath and pushed open the door. Maggie darted in ahead of me; I heard the bed groan as she leapt onto it. I reached for the light switch holding my breath once again. As light washed over the room, I instantly was transported back to high school. The room hadn't changed a tiny bit. His walls were still the pale blue we had painted them sophomore year in high school. His letterman jacket was still hanging on the back of his desk chair. Every photograph he had framed in high school still sat exactly where they were put all those years ago. Even the bedding was the same. I had made him a quilt for his sixteenth birthday. It was made out of vintage tee shirts, and it took up residence on his bed that night. Twelve years later it still covered the queen sized bed.

" Some things never change Maggie. " I smiled as I climbed into bed next to her. I covered us both up with the quilt and lay listening to her quiet snore. My conversation with Madison continued to replay in my head. I didn't want to admit it but maybe she was right. Maybe a small part of me was still in love with Brandon. I didn't want to be, and I do think he is an asshole. But you don't ever truly fall out of love with your first love, do you? I mean first love is always that life changing can't eat, can't sleep consuming feeling. You will never be in love like that again, because it is the only time you will fall in love unconditionally, unjaded, and without expectations of the fear and pain love can cause. So yeah a tiny part of what she said could be right. But that is only because a small part of me will always be in love with Brandon. However a much larger part of me currently hates him. Maggie snuggled her head into the crook of my neck drawing me back to the present, and the fact that I was attempting to go to sleep in a bed I spent so many secret nights in growing up.

I was still awake when Brandon came stumbling into the house hours later. I lay in bed spooning with Maggie, there was no point in getting up he was drunk, and probably not alone. The door cracked open, his body leaned against the doorframe for support.

" Pige you still up." He whispered.

" Yeah, your dog snores like an eighty year old man, with a serious sinus infection." I whispered back. He opened the door wider and swayed across the room. " You a little drunk?" I teased as he stumbled over his own two feet.

" Yeah, just a little. Slide over Pige." He stood next to the bed, waiting for me to move closer to Maggie so he had room to lie down.

" Brandon I don't think that is a good idea." I averted my eyes, turning back towards the door. I felt him inch down onto the bed. His breath was hot on my neck.

" Come on Pige, just snuggle with me for old times sake. I had a bad night and just want to spoon." His body lay pressed against my back. I knew he was barley on the bed. I sighed heavily and inched closer to Maggie. Brandon readjusted in the bed, throwing his arm across my waist, while tucking my head under his chin. I felt myself go ridged as his finger traced my hip bone.

" Why was it a bad night?" I asked, desperately trying to figure out how to get out of this situation.

" Candy kind of ripped me a new asshole about blowing her off for you last night. It's really not that big of a deal." He trailed off. She kept going on and on about how I have you on a pedestal and no one else will ever compare. She called you a dick tease and a bitch. So we broke up. Man that girl went crazy throwing shit, hell she broke my head light and mirror off my truck with a baseball bat. I don't get it I have made it eminently clear that we were not serious, but that crazy woman had it in her head that we were getting married. I don't get why these women I date can't get it thru their heads there was only ever one girl I wanted to" His voice trailed off, and his arm had become dead weight against my hip.   There was no way I was going to get any sleep tonight. I was sandwiched between him and the dog. Trying to pretend he hadn't just told me all of that. I wanted to wake him up and ask him to finish his sentence. Even though I know damn right well I can't handle what he almost said. Tomorrow morning I would act like none of this had happened. He was so drunk he was never going to remember.

CHAPTER NINE
Elizabeth

I set a cup of coffee on the nightstand the next morning while Maggie jumped all over the bed.

" Rise and shine drunky." I said with a laugh when he finally opened his eyes.

" Did I do anything stupid last night?" He sat up clutching his head.

" From what I understand you dodged a bullet with some crazy girl who damaged your truck, and you passed out in here. Mumbling something about old time sake." I tried to act nonchalant. Our eyes met, and we silently verified that we both knew I was lying. Yet neither one of us said a word about what actually was said last night. It was easier that way. In fact, I don't honestly think he meant everything he said last night. He had been extremely drunk and just swept up in the nostalgia of first love.

" Give me twenty minutes and I'll be ready to go okay. If you don't want to sit out back all day you can just stay here." He mumbled as he climbed out of bed.

" I'll be fine. Actually I think I'm going to crash at Madison's tonight. She want to have a girls night so it will just be easier to pass out on her couch." I watched the disappointment flash across his face for just a second before he his poker face returned.

" That makes sense. I should be able to replace all of the support beams today. I have a friend coming to help out. So tomorrow I can get the base for the floor down. So you will be able to sleep there tomorrow night. " He brushed past me, on his way to the bathroom. There was nothing to say in response. I needed to distance myself from Brandon before I got hurt again, or hurt him again. I wasn't going to stay here forever, I couldn't I had been here a few days and already I could feel the small town suffocating me.

Neither one of us spoke on the way to my house. In fact, it was the longest ten-minute car ride of my life. I knew he was hurt about me not wanting to stay at his house tonight. Which if you ask me is ridiculous. I should be the one who is pissed. Who was he to climb in bed with me last night, even after I had protested? Okay, okay so I didn't put up that much of a fight. In fact, it had been nice to have a warm body next to mine, for about half a second. Then he started talking. If he had just kept his stupid drunk mouth shut then I could have pretended everything was fine. But no he had to start talking. He had to rip bandages off of wounds that would never fully heal. So he had no right to be pissed. But I do. Just like I was the one who needed to put some serious distance between the two of us before the wounds ended up to vast to ever bandage shut again. Not that, he cared. He didn't care when he had created them the first time, and he sure as hell wasn't going to care now.

The car jerked to a stop in front of my house, and Brandon was out and slamming the car door before the car had even fully stopped. I climbed out shutting the door as quietly as possible. He wanted a fight, and I was not about to give him one. Instead, I calmly walked my bags into the house, before leaving just as quietly as I had come in. I walked down the street towards the elementary school. I knew Madison would be dropping her oldest off at first grade in about five minutes. I couldn't sit in my back yard all day listening to Brandon slamming things inside. Instead, I would hide out in Madison's kitchen. Spending the day with my best friend and one of my two godchildren would be a perfect distraction.

" Aunt Wizzy, Aunt Wizzy, we got you offee. Mama said you would obly be here." The curly haired three year old came tearing down the sidewalk towards me. She launched her self into my arms when she finally reached me.

" Your Mommy is a very smart lady." I kissed her forehead as I shifted her onto my hip.

" Morning sunshine, I cleaned off the kitchen table last night for you." Madison said as she handed me a take out cup of coffee.

" Was that before or after you called me a bitch for hanging up on you." Apologies were never needed in our friendship. All that is required is truing it into a joke.

" It was long after I called you a bitch. Jim came home from the bar and said he had run into Brandon and some chick fighting. Said he heard your name a few times, then she stormed out, and he sat at the bar muttering about how you were at home sleeping in his childhood bed. So I figured you were either going to end up on my couch last night, or hiding out in my kitchen today." She threw her arm around my shoulder steering me down the street towards her house. If Jim her husband had come home from the bar last night and rattled all of that off, I'm sure they both were praying I'd end up there last night. They both loved a good drama filled story, and last night had the potential to be drama filled.

" Well apparently he got really pissed because Candice wanted to get all kinds of serious with him. Which he didn't want. He was mumbling about how she couldn't get it thru her head that he was never going to marry her, and there was only ever one girl who he wanted to. He never finished that sentence because he passed out. He also insisted in sleeping in bed with me. He isn't talking to me today because I told him I was having a girl's night with you tonight, and staying at your house. Madison I just don't understand what the hell is going on." I sunk into one of the two arondeck chairs in her back yard.

" Abby you go play like a good girl while Mommy and Aunt Wizzy talk okay?" We both watched as the little girl ran across the yard towards the sand box.

" Iz, regardless of what you want to hear. I think you both still have feeling for each other. I don't think either of you ever really got closure. Hell I don't even know what really happened in the end, no one does as a matter of fact." She stared at me waiting for the explanation eight years in the making.

" Oh Madison it's a really long story." I sighed, knowing damn right well she didn't care it the story took two weeks to tell.

" Well then I guess it's a good thing I just put on more coffee. Out with it, I can't give you advice, or even begin to figure out what is going on with the two of you if you don't share the back story." She tucked her legs under her, and settled in looking very much like a kindergarten waiting for story time to start.

" How much do you know Madison?" I was secretly hoping she knew more then she had let on that would save me a lot of time.

" I know that the two of you spent a lot of time together. Both of you never really dated anyone else during high school. No one ever knew if you and Brandon were an item. I know that the water tower has some secret meaning to the two of you, and last night I finally got you to admit that you lost your virginity to him on top of that water tower." She sheepishly grinned.

" You tricked me into admitting that last night?" I screeched.

" Actually Brandon told Jim about it a year ago during a drunken game of pool. So all I did was get you to admit it last night." She shrugged her shoulders. " Are you going to spill it or what?" She reached over and took a large drink out of her coffee. While I was debating about how I was going to kill Brandon, and his inability to keep his mouth shut and his feelings under control when he was drunk.

" Yes, but you have to contain your questions until I'm done, other wise we really be here until next week." I said, I knew Madison well, and that girl was not only impatient, but had to ask a question about everything.

" I will do my best." She held up her hand, making the sign of Spock from Star Trek. " Scout Honor."

" You dumb ass, that is not from the girl scouts. That is from Star Trek. Regardless let me start before I decide spending the day with Brandon storming around my house is a better idea. Up until freshman year in high school Brandon and I had a serious love hate relationship."

" Until freshman year, girl that is some serious bullshit you have had that relationship since the three of us met in kindergarten." Madison interrupted.

" Whatever Madison, like I was saying. Everything kind of change during the home coming dance. You don't have any idea what went down that night because you and Jim were out back of the gym with your tongues shoved down each other throats. (Yes, that is correct Madison and Jim are high school sweethearts, haven't ever dated anyone else, and never wanted to kind of couple.) Well I showed up with Brad Anderson."

" Oh my god did you know he has six kids, all with different mothers?"

" Madison you are killing me. When I said no questions, I was trying to avoid eighteen hundred interruptions. Once again like I was saying Brad Anderson was my date. I was so excited as he was a grade older, and the dreamiest boy in the whole school. With his dusty blond hair, emerald green eyes and washboard abs. Before you ask yes I know he is now fat and bald. Well he kept trying to get me to go into one of the empty classrooms with him. I didn't want to go. I hadn't even had my first kiss yet, and he was all over me, pawing at my butt, and trying to grab my boobs. I excused myself to go the bathroom, and he followed me. The second we got into the empty hallway he was trying to drag me into the nearest door. I was begging him to let me go, he was pulling on my arm so hard I had bruises for days. I didn't even know Brandon was coming to the dance. Just as I was starting to panic and cry there Brandon was stepping out of the shadows.

"Yo dude the lady said let her go." I heard him before I saw him and instantly felt relieved. Brad course didn't let me go instead he told Brandon to but out. In all honestly, the only real part of that conversation was when Brandon first spoke. There was some more of a verbal exchange between the two of them. Before I knew it Brandon had his arm wrapped around my waist, and the other arm was punching Brad square in the face. That broken jaw and nose Brad had refused to tell anyone how he got. Yeah that was Brandon, and he did it one handed, because his other hand as busy pulling me behind him." I looked over at Madison her eyes were giant round saucers, and her coffee cup hung in mid air. I could tell she was dying to say something, anything.

" The dance was only an hour in, and I couldn't go home yet, not with three hours left in the dance. Nan would have known something was wrong if I went home that early. So after Brandon took my hand and lead me very quickly out of the school, before we were both in trouble for what happened to Brads face, we ended up at the water tower. We hadn't spoken until after we were both sitting on the top of the tower. I turned towards him to thank him, and before I could he kissed me. We sat on the tower talking after that until after midnight. It was the first of many nights on top of the water tower. Yes, I also lost my virginity to him on top of that tower. The night before I left for college he carved B+P = 4 ever into the railing. It's still there. We were never actually a couple, I mean we didn't date other people, but we were never officially boyfriend and girlfriend. We both admitted that we were in love with each other, and that was enough for us. But clearly love wasn't enough to make it work once I left for college. It started out we talked multiple times a day, and then it drifted down to once a day and slowly every other day. He had been saying he was going to come up for a long weekend and see me. It was Halloween weekend, and I was sitting in a bar just off campus, the bar we agreed to meet in. He was over an hour late, and not answering his cell phone. By midnight, he was four hours late. I stood up to leave and ran directly into Jonathan. I tried to get a hold of Brandon for the next two weeks, but he wouldn't return my phone calls. After that, I just stopped trying, and until two days ago him and I haven't spoken since two days before he blew me off."

" You haven't asked him why he didn't show up?" That was the one question I wasn't expecting to come out of Madison's mouth.

" No, Madison it doesn't matter why he didn't show up. One minute he is promising me forever, and the next he is disappearing from my life without so much as a good-bye" I replied.

" Iz I think you need to ask him why he didn't come." Madison stood up and started towards her kitchen.

" Madison Marie what do you know? What have you been keeping from me? I could feel my blood pressure rising. All these years I have spend wondering what I did wrong, and she knew. She knows why he didn't come and she still is refusing to tell me.

" You need to ask him." She turned away from me. I didn't

bother to tell her I was leaving. Instead I stormed out her front door. I was planning on asking him because clearly everyone else already knew why he didn't come. He could make sure my best friend knew why, and yet he couldn't tell me. Oh hell no, I wanted answers and I was about to get them. I cut through back yards, and jay walked across the street, taking the fastest way possible to my house.

When I finally turned the corner onto my street, his truck was still in the driveway. I threw open my front door and almost knocked over the ladder he was standing on.

" Jesus Pige watch where you are going." Brandon shot down at me. Clearly he was still pissed.

" Brandon why didn't you come to Boston?" I kicked his ladder trying to get his attention.

" Pige can we do this another time?" His anger was radiating through his voice.

" No, we can talk about this now, or I can kick over the ladder and refuse to get you medical attention until you tell me." I screamed at him.

" Fine you want to do this here. I did come to Boston. I got there I walked around and then I turned around and came home. I was standing outside of the bar for two hours that night, and I watched you try to call me. Pige I got to the city and I walked through your campus, and I realized I was nothing more then some small town country boy. You had become a high fashion, classy city girl over night. I couldn't compete. Just like there was no way I could ever live somewhere I couldn't see the stars at night, where the traffic never stops, or where is more pavement then grass. You on the other hand loved it in the city. You never wanted to live anywhere else. So Yeah Pige I came and I took one look at the girl I loved and decided you could have a better life if I just bowed out." His face was inches from mine. I reached out and slapped him, without even thinking.

" You broke my heart, you shattered it into a million little pieces because you decided you knew what was best for me? I have spent the last eight years pretending I was over you, and hating you. All because you decided it wouldn't work without ever talking to me? You know what screw you Brandon. Do not ever speak to me again. Finish this damn project as quickly as possible and then get the hell out of my life." I turned and stormed out of the house. I had no idea where the hell I was going. My house looked like a war zone, I wasn't speaking to my best friend, and I didn't want to talk to my grandmother. There was only one place left to go, the water tower.

I woke up hours later on top of the water tower. It was to sound of music that had woken me up. I reached for my cell phone only to discover it was dead.

" Pigeon, I am sorry for breaking your heart eight years ago. I talked to Madison. I had no idea me breaking your heart pushed you into Jonathan's arms. Pige, please forgive me., I let you leave my life once. I can't let you walk out of my life a second time. " He was screaming over the song that had been playing the first time he told me he loved me. I stood up and carefully climbed down the ladder. I reached the bottom and just stood staring at him. Neither of us said anything for what felt like an eternity.

" Bran I'm sorry I slapped you and told you to get out of my life. I never wanted you to leave in the first place. But I need you to understand we can't pick up were we left off when we were eight teen. Hell I don't even think we can be anything more than friends right now. I'm broken, like damaged beyond repair broken, and I can't open my heart up again anytime soon. I don't know if I ever want to be romantically involved with anyone again." Brandon pressed his fingers to my lips.

" I know Pige, all I am asking for is a chance to be in your life again. If all you can handle is friends, then I will accept friends. I just know that I can't live without you in my life. I had no idea how miserable I had been these last eight years until I was standing on your door step staring into you hazel eyes." He shrugged his shoulders, his face strewn with worry. I took one timid step forward, then another until I was inches from him. I threw my arms around his waist and pulled him tight against my body.

" Thanks for understanding B. Is the offer for your guest bedroom still open?" I tilted my head up to look at his face.

" Of course it is movies and junk food in bed, like when we were kids?" He pulled back, keeping just one arm wrapped around my shoulders.

" I'll even let you pick the movies."

" Good because tomorrow night your room will be done, so I deserve to pick it solely because of how hard I worked today." He opened the door to his truck letting me slide in. I wasn't used to having someone so readily and easily accepting what I needed, or even understanding everything I wasn't saying. Friendship was going to be difficult because a seriously large part of me was still in love with him. But I couldn't trust him, or myself to make it work. His reasons for not walking into that bar all those years ago would stop him from walking into the bar today too. So for now I would enjoy the moments of friendship because sooner or later all I will have are the memories to bring me brief moments of joy.

CHAPTER TEN
Brandon

She sat curled up next to me, tucked into my side with her head on my chest watching the movie. Like sitting damn near on my lap was perfectly normal. Maybe it once had been, but not today, not this week, not this year, hell it didn't even feel like it had been normal in this lifetime. I had accepted years ago that our love story was not going to be an epic novel. No instead it was nothing more than a brief essay, a life-changing essay in my world. But an essay just the same. That was until a few days ago when she opened the front door of the re-model Nan had asked me to do. Just like that she was walking back into my life, and turning my world upside down without any kind of warning. When a girl like Pige is going to walk into you life, trust me, you need a hell of a lot more than some bull shit caution sign. You are going to need a fucking tsunami warning, with bells, whistles, and nothing but that warning on every TV station. Even with a warning of that magnitude there is no way you will escape hurricane Pigeon unscathed. Especially if you are me.

No, one look in her hazel eyes, and I was struggling to keep my head above water. I was instantly back in

Mandelyn Kilroy

kindergarten when she walked into the classroom, her chocolate cherry hair tied up in two pigtails with to pink bows, a pink skirt, and white tee shirt. Yes, I remember what she was wearing the first day of kindergarten, I can tell you what she was wearing the first time I kissed her, told her I loved her, and the day I stood her up in the bar in Boston. Those were some of the most significant days of my life. That day in Boston had been the day my life ended. I just couldn't actually die like I wanted to. Instead, I had to live a meaningless existence that I filled with anything to distract me from wondering how she was.

    Then like a serious ass last night, I had left her sitting in my house, so I could go out with Candice. I could have told Pige that it wasn't anything serious. It never had been and never would be. Instead, I walked out and let her make her own assumptions. Why? Because I am an asshole, and I seriously fucked up last night. I had come up with this grand plan about how I was going to win her back, and in a matter of minute, I had flushed it down the crapper. But I couldn't just leave it as a small screw up easily fixable. Nope that would make my life easy. Instead, I had broken up with Candice in the parking lot of Jake's like I had planned on. She had cried and whined in some pathetic attempt to change my mind. When that didn't work, her being the classy person she is, she dropped to her knees and attempted to change my mind. I walked away and left her on her knees. I should have gone home immediately before there was a chance of anymore damage happening. What did I do? I went inside and got drunk because it was easier than going home and fighting the urge to pin Pige against a wall and make her scream my name.

    That damn bitch Candice clearly did not appreciate being left on her knees. Which isn't truely my problem, seeing how I never told her to get on her damn knees. While we are on this topic, I don't understand how she thought a blow job was going to change my mine. Well had I just gone home and fought my urges there wouldn't have been any new rumors floating around town. Rumors that will make their way back to Pige and just throw an even bigger wrench into my plans. While she hasn't said anything I know Jim was at the bar, and more than likely was calling his wife while it went down. Long story short, Candice felt the need to come barrel assin into the bar, screaming about what a home wrecking bitch my Pigeon is. Screaming about how she turned her husband gay, and now me as well. It wasn't the gay comment that got me. It was her calling my girl a bitch. Yeah okay so she is not my girl right this very minute. But believe you me she will be. I snapped, called her the most unbecoming word in the world. I swear on everything holy it was the first time the c word has ever left my lips. Then I dumped a pitcher of beer on her head, and told her the reason I told her to get off her knees in the parking lot was because she was the worst sex of my life.

    This about the time I stumbled home, only to discover my traitor of a dog was curled up in the exact place I had wanted to be. In my drunken stupor I decided she was only going to be in my house for one or two nights, so I might as well give it a shot. I didn't want anything more than to hold her. I had spent the last eight years trying to forget every night how she felt in my arms. Every night I tossed and turned unable to forget how her head felt on my chest, or how her sighs had become my lullaby. Truthfully the last thing I needed for my own sanity was to lie down next to her. Yet my body took over, and as I held her against my chest, it was like nothing had changed. I couldn't stop myself. I started to tell her about the bar. I couldn't shut up, or make the words stop coming. In the end, I pretended to be asleep a moment before I finished the sentence that was sure to ruin every chance I had of her even considering us being friends again. I had almost told her that she was the only girl I had ever wanted and will ever want to marry. Yeah that sentence is sure to make any woman run for the hills. Let alone a woman whose husband left her a little over a month ago. I couldn't tell her how I felt about her. How I had always felt about her. Which is why I continue to refuse to explain the nickname she hated for so many years. That is just another truth that would cause her to run clear across the country. I had let her run to Boston once, and didn't even know how to fight for her then. I couldn't let her run a second time. Instead, I was going to have to bite my tongue and try my damnedest to prove that I'm not the same person who let her walk away all those years ago.

    Which will probably explain why I am sitting on my couch watching Guys and Dolls. While she is sound asleep on my chest, with the remote tucked down at the other end of the couch. She looks to peaceful to move, and I am terrified that if she wakes up this moment I have been craving since her last night at home will be over. She had made it unquestionably clear she wasn't even sure she could handle anything more than casual friends right now. So I needed to savor every moment like this I can before she decides she can't handle having me in her life. I carefully pulled the quilt on the back of the couch down and over her, as I propped my feet up on the coffee table. I had no plans for moving and if this was where she felt comfortable enough to sleep then by god I would spend the night watching her peacefully sleep with her head on my chest. She would never believe me, but right now in this moment, when she has no makeup on, and her hair is piled up in a messy blob on the top of her head. When she is lounging in my old high school sweatshirt, and a pair of my boxer shorts. This is when I find her the most beautiful. Right now is when she truly takes my breath away.

    Tomorrow I was going to find some other reason as to why she couldn't stay in her house. Some other tiny issue that

From here to forever

I was going to blow way out of proportion. Like the wood floors under the carpet that honestly just needed to be ripped up. There was nothing wrong with her support beams, or the ceiling in her first floor. But it had guaranteed I would be around for a few more days, and allow me some more alone time with her. Of course, it was costing me money. A decent amount of it. She didn't know it yet, but I wasn't planning on charging her anything over what the original quote for the job had been. That quote had actually been for Nan the only woman in the world I am terrified of, and loved fiercely at the same time. That quote hadn't been much more then the cost of materials, I had known I would been eating some of the labor costs, but now I was going to be eating at least ten grand in labor and materials by the time the project was done. I couldn't rightfully charge either of them over something that was a bold faced lie. I may stretch the truth to get what I want, but I am not a rip off.

CHAPTER ELEVEN
Elizabeth

I had gotten the phone call exactly one week ago from Jonathan's assistant. Politely informing me that not only had the house sold but that the mediation for the division of assets was going to be held in one week. I had the option to send my legal counsel, or I could choose to attend myself. I had sat there in shock staring at the phone long after the call had ended. Two months ago I had been in what I thought was a happy, and healthy marriage. Now the house I had spent years turning into a home was no longer mine, and my marriage was about to become nothing more than a non valid certificate. To make matters even worse I had not even begun to think about legal counsel. I've had a lawyer since I was handed my first publishing contract. While my lawyer is phenomenal and has negotiated my book contracts for the last eight years. He knows nothing about divorce. Besides I couldn't send someone else in my place, Jonathan works for one of the biggest legal firms in Boston, anyone I send would not only get blindsided, but would get me screwed. Instead, I decided that it would be best if I went and handled this on my own.

    I am going to be completely honest at this point in time. When I made the decision, I had consumed an entire bottle of wine, and was lying fully clothed in my empty bathtub. When I get terribly drunk, and I mean drunk to the point of not being able stand up because your head is spinning like you just spun in circles for twenty minutes. I like to lay in the bath tub. You can't fall out of the bathtub, once you are laying down, which always makes me feel just a little safer when I am as intoxicated as I was that night. I guess I should explain, I don't actually drink. Like ever. One glass of wine makes me tipsy, so an entire bottle is enough to make me pray to the porcelain gods.

So like, I was saying. In my drunken stupor I e-mailed his assistant back and told her I would be coming in person for the mediation, and to sign off on any paper work for the house. Before I sent this e-mail, which I re-read the next morning, when I was sober. I am actually proud of my drunken e-mail, not only was it politically correct, but grammatically correct, and there wasn't a single spelling error. I had a extraordinarily long conversation with my body wash, shampoo, and conditioner. Listen there was no one else to talk to at 2 in the morning. The four of us decided that I needed to go back to Boston and face Jonathan myself. That it would provide me with the closure I needed. The closure was not my idea, because as far as I was concerned closure wasn't something I was ever truly going to get. But my mint shampoo can be a stubborn bitch when she puts her foot down.

Which is how I ended up standing in a hotels bathroom, trying my best to look irresistible. I was still holding out even the tiniest bit of hope that he would take one look at me, fall to his knees and beg me to take him back. This tiny bit of hope is the reason I had refused all offers for company or moral support, as my Nana and brother had called it. I glanced at my cell phone. It was ten minutes to nine, which meant I needed to leave now. Jonathan's office was directly across the street. But I still needed to check out and put my overnight bag in my car, and still be to the tenth floor of his officer by nine. I took one last look at my self in the mirror; I was exceptionally close to inappropriate. My hair was loosely curled, settling down around my shoulders, I had decided to wear a cream sweater dress. It was a scoop neck, which hung suggestively low, revealing a tiny bit to much cleavage. Which looked much larger than normal thanks to a new push up bra which promised to add two cup sizes. It lived up to it's promise. The dress rested just above my knee and hugged my ass like a second skin. I had never been over weight, but four weeks ago when my husband told me he wanted a divorce I would have needed spanks to make my stomach look this flat, and my ass that toned. But thanks to the divorce diet, I had lost the ten pounds I had been trying to lose for the last two years. Who knew all I needed to do to lose my tummy pouch was get divorced. I slide my lace ankle booties on, and the diamond solitaire my grandmother had given me when I graduated college around my neck, before walking out of the room.

Thirty minutes later I was sitting in front of the receptionist desk, which was where I had been sitting for the last twenty-two minutes. I was starting to get pissed, and I knew damn right well that this was all part of his game. He seemed to forget telling me all about this tactic over dinner a hundred times.

" Keep them waiting exactly thirty minutes. It will annoy them. Which means they will come in a little pissed, rather than cool, calm and collected. It makes them easier to push over." He would say his mouth full of food. A habit that always made my stomach turn. That and this annoying slapping slurping sound he made when he chewed his food. I glanced at my watch, 9:29. I took a deep breath, refusing to go in there pissed. I was not going to let him walk all over me.

" Ms. Cole you can follow me." His receptionist stood up

motioning for me to follow her down the hallway. I shook my head she had been at my house for dinner just a few months ago. When the hell did I become Ms. Cole? While we are on this formality issue, when did I start getting called by my maiden name? Now was not the time to think about this issue. He had just made it clear he was going to play dirty. Damn it I should have hired a lawyer to deal with this. My shampoo and I were going to have a extremely long talk about how much her advice just royally fucked me the next time I get drunk. Which would probably be tonight when I got home. I squared my shoulder, before entering the room.

" Elizabeth, it lovely to see you." Dan, Jonathan's boss smiles across the table from me. With one swift motion, he gestured for me to have a seat across from him, and took his seat.

" Daniel, it's lovely to see you as well. Such a shame it has to be under these circumstances. Hello Jonathan." I looked at my husband for the first time since I had watched him walk out of our house, that terrible morning.

" Lizzie, you look wonderful." He smiled at me, and for the first time since we had met in Jakes bar, all those years ago I didn't get the familiar flutter in my stomach. I ignored his compliment, silently applauding my dress choice.

" Daniel, since out meeting is already starting thirty minutes late, do you mind if we skip the chit chat and get down to business?" All kindness had left my voice; I was pure business at this point in time.

" Yes of course, I am sure you have already reviewed the offer on the house?" He slid the offer across the desk. I had received it six days ago via e-mail. I knew what it said.

" Yes I have reviewed the offer, and even though it is ten thousand less then our asking price, I am willing to sell at that cost, with one stipulation. I want a thirty day settlement, not a sixty day settlement." If they wanted to continue to treat me like I was a child, I was going to start making my demands before they started playing hardball.

" I'm sure that will not be a problem for Devon." Jonathan smirked as he dropped the bomb that his tiny, twenty-two year old, bleach blond, size two, fake boobed receptionist was buying my house. I wanted to cry on the spot, fighting desperately to keep my composure.

" What else is there to wrap up? I would prefer not to waste more time than necessary here." In walked the little tramp, just as I was finishing my sentence. She placed a tray of coffee down on the table while the men discussed a thirty-day settlement. I was so angry my pulse was pounding in my ears, making it impossible to pay attention to what they say. Both men smiled as she walked out of the office, so I am assuming she said yes.

" Back to your question, there is the division of assets, the vacation house, as well as the boat, the stocks, the bonds, and the IRA." I held my hand up cutting Daniel off.

" I know what assets we have. However clearly your client has not informed you that I was never stupid enough to make my assets join. So he can keep the joint assets, he was the only one contributing to them. He can also shove the boat up his ass, and if he wants the vacation house he can buy my half from me. Other wise I want it sold. Now I do believe that is everything correct." I shoved my chair back, and ripped the door open. Pausing to look both men in the eyes. " I expect the divorce paper, and a check for my half of both houses in my hands in no less then sixty days. Have a wonderful day gentle men." I stormed across the office frantically pushing the elevator button. My anger was giving way to tears I didn't want to cry.

" Lizzie, I'm sorry." I don't understand how this bitch was smart enough to buy a house because she clearly had no common sense.

Mandelyn Kilroy

Common sense would have told her to keep her mouth shut. No, no, not her. Her's told her to come stand next to me, and attempt to comfort me.

" It's Ms. Cole Devon, and your sorry for what, for screwing my husband, or buying my home? What are you sorry for you snotty little bitch?" Like I said common sense should have told her to keep her mouth shut. I climbed into the elevator sickly enjoying the shock plastered across her face, as the asshole I once called husband ran for the elevator. I watched the door slam shut in his face. I had nothing left to say to him, and clearly he had no common sense either. My god they are fucking perfect for each other. If he had gotten in this elevator with me, I would have murdered him, and blood is impossible to get out of cream-colored cashmere. The elevator door opened on the ground floor, and I should have known not to bask in the thought of getting out of here without him catching me. There, he stood doubled over gasping for breath.

" You are kidding me right? I mean this is a joke correct. Some hidden camera is going to pop out any second right? For the love of god, you told me you wanted a divorce. Well that's a lie, you blind sided me, after waking me up so you could get laid and start you work week off right, with the news that you were divorcing me, and moving out of the house immediately, and now you are running down ten flights of stairs after me. What the hell is your deal?" I couldn't help but yell.

" Lizzie just let me explain." He pled; I think it was a pitiful attempt as getting me under control.

" Let you explain? What is it that you need to explain, how your screwing your secretary? How she is buying the house? Mother fucker I know what you pay her and it's not enough for a half a million-dollar house. So let me guess your going to explain, how she is buying the house, and once the divorce is done you are putting it in both of your name right? Well don't worry wouldn't want to make it any harder on the two of you. You can save your selves some time and just do it the right way." I could feel a rouge tear trickle down my cheek as everyone in the foyer stopped to stare at us.

" Baby, look there was so much I wanted to give you. But I couldn't." He reached his hand towards me, in yet another attempt to soothe me. I wanted to snap his hand off of his arm, and then bitch slap him with it.

" Excuse me, you know what John you keep telling your self that. If it helps you sleep at night. Hate is a strong word, and I want you to know I really really dislike you right now. Do you know what I saw when I looked at you in that office earlier? I no longer saw the amazing man I married. The man who once gave me butterflies, who could take my breath away with one look. No, instead I saw some pathetic, insecure, scared little boy. I honestly have no idea what I ever saw in you, or what I ever liked about you as a matter of fact. I hope she screws you over, and I hope you lay awake reliving how this right here has been the biggest mistake of your life." I pushed past him and sprinted towards the exit. I no longer cared if I looked like an ass. At least fifty people had just witnessed me calling out Jonathan.

" Elizabeth stop." I pushed the door open, trying to pretend I didn't hear him calling my name. I silently thanked god that I had parked right out front of the building. I grabbed my keys from my purse and looked up trying to get my bearings thru my tears.

" I said stop." I felt his hand wrap around my arm as he spun me around to face him. For a split second, I wish I had agreed to let someone come with me. "Jesus, you can't behave like this, you can't be this much of a bitch. What the hell is wrong with you?" He was screaming in my face as his other hand grabbed my free arm, before I could slap him.

" I suggest you let her go Jonathan." My eyes went wide with shock. There was no way Brandon was here. I should have sent a lawyer in my place because today was clearly the breaking point for my sanity. " I said you should let her go." His breath hit the back of my neck, in a warm rush of comfort. I hadn't lost my mind; he was actually here in Boston. He had been waiting against my car waiting for me. Maybe just maybe he wasn't as awful as I thought.

" Listen buddy, stop trying to be a hero and walk away, I'm in the middle of having a conversation with my wife." Jonathan said over my shoulder, shooting death glares in Brandon's direction.

" Jonathan from what I understand, you decided you wanted a divorce. Which means she isn't your wife. So I'm going to ask you one more time, and if you don't do what I ask I am going to forcefully remove your hands from her body. Let her go." A shiver ran down my spine. As Brandon's threat caused the hands wrapped around my arms loosen. I ripped my arms from his grip and turned to run. I took half a step and found my self crushed against Brandon's chest.

" You okay Pige?" I nodded my head against his chest no longer trusting my voice. " Jonathan you never should have left her if you couldn't let her go. If couldn't see stand to see her in someone else arms, or scroll by her number and not call her, then your never should have let her go." Brandon turned keeping me tucked into his chest. My eyes were still clammed shut. I knew he was leading me to my car; I still had no idea what he was doing here or how he got here. All that mattered right now, was he had come, and was unknowingly keeping me my head above water. We stopped, and I felt him turn once more. I opened my eyes breathing a sigh of relief when I discovered he had tucked me behind him allowing me to lean against the car and still be sheltered. " One more thing Jonathan, when you finally wake up and realize what you have

From here to forever

lost. When you realize you have lost more than just some girl who turns every head when she walks down the sidewalk. The girl who can cause a traffic accident when she is dressed in over sized sweet pants and ratty college tee shirt. Don't come looking for her." Brandon took a step forward, separating our bodies, and I almost whimpered in protest. His finger was inches from Jonathan's face. " Because you will have to go thru me to get to her, and that's not a fight I am going to loss." He turned around sliding his hand around my waist while opening the passengers door. He slid me into the car before walking around to the drives door, pausing one last time to shoot a death glare at Jonathan. He slid into the drivers seat and started the car. Neither one of us spoke until we has hit the highway out of town. The silence was killing me, and in all honesty I kind of wanted to be alone, so I could cry in my steering wheel right now.

" You can get off at the next exit, so we can circle back to get your car." I point to the sign that informed us the next exit was in 1.5 miles.

" Pige my car is parked in your driveway. So there is no need to get off at the next exit unless you need to go back for something. I'm sorry I didn't even ask if you were ready to go home." He glanced at me out of the corner of his eye. His concern pulled at the corner of his lips, I wanted to reach out and reassure him.

" No, there is nothing I need or want left in that city. I just want to go back to Middleton." The silence settled over the car again as the truth in my words hung in the air, mixing with the questions neither of us were vocalizing. I sat staring out the window, watching the distance grow between my home or ex home and myself. I don't even know what to call Boston anymore. Other then a city that I love, whose memory will remain tainted because of its association with the moment my perfect world shattered down around me. It was a city, who's siren song no longer called to me, a realization that left me emptier than the person I had vowed forever to leaving me.

"Pigeon are you okay." His quiet question broke into my thoughts, dragging me back into the present, and forcing me to shake off the sadness that was slowly over taking me again.

" Yeah I'm fine." I muttered, letting my headrest against the window.

" I'm calling bullshit, you haven't said a word in the last two hours. Hell you haven't even asked me why I was there, or called me over bearing, or an asshole, or read me the riot act for ignoring your wishes. Come on out with it. I've been patiently waiting for the grand speech that I know is coming. About how you are an independent woman not a damsel in distress, and the last thing you need is some wanna be knight rushing in to rescue you." The car abruptly came to a stop. I lifted my eyes from my lap and realized that he had pulled into a rest stop, and we were indeed over almost three hours from Boston. " We are not moving until you spill it." He turned off the car, shoving the car keys in the door next to him, before shifting in the seat to face me. I was getting downright pissed at anyone who owned a penis today. Who the hell does he think he is? He came swooping in like some super hero, and now he is no better then the idiot he had saved me from. Yes, he is not physically holding me here in an attempt to make me talk. He is still forcing me to talk, and to think not that long ago I had honestly thought he wasn't as bad as I had thought. Well I retract that statement his he worse. Between me you and the wall, while I am pissed at him, and can't believe I honestly thought he was half decent a few hours ago, I was a little turned on at him behaving like a domesticated caveman while trying to protect me.

" Fine Brandon lets talk. Why the hell were you in Boston, and how did you get there without your car?" I forced the words out of my mouth, scouring at the bitter taste they left behind. If I didn't know he was dead serious, I would have sat in silence until he got pissed and continued home. But I know Brandon, and if I didn't start talking we would still be sitting her next week. However he only told me I needed to start talking. He said nothing about looking at him, so I will not avert my eyes from the crack in the pavement just outside of my window.

" I was thinking about our conversation from the other day, yesterday afternoon. The more I thought about it the more I was worried he was going to give you a hard time. So I booked a seat on a red eye and left for the airport very early this morning. Thankfully the plane ride from Philly to Boston is short. I landed at nine this morning, so I grabbed a cab to the lawyers office, and stood outside against your car until you came out. I saw you running out the door in tears, but before I could even say your name he was grabbing you. In all honesty, it took everything in my power not to knock him on his ass the second he touched you. Do you want to talk about why you were in tears?" I turned towards him, forgetting my resolution of looking nowhere but out my window. I was dumb founded over what he had just confessed. His expression took my breath away for just a moment. The blue eyes that I swore saw directly into my soul were filled with unadulterated hatred. Yet his brows were creased with worry and concern. There was a hint of something I couldn't place hiding in the corners of his eyes and mouth. If I didn't know better I would say it was hints of love.

" You got on a plane in the middle of the night, flew into the Boston, and then took a cab to the lawyers officer. In hopes that you could find me or my car because you were worried?" I had to say it out loud. Just to see if it sounded as crazy when I said it, as it did when he had just explained it. He shrugged his shoulders in response, nodding his head yes ever so slightly. " Brandon, thank you." I leaned forward brushing my lips across his check.

" You're thanking me? Pige I'm really a concerned about your mental state. Where is the lecture, and the how dare you?"

" Brandon, there is no lecture. Yes, I don't do damsel in distress well, and yes it is even harder to admit when I need moral support, or any kind of help for that matter. But today I needed it, and I didn't even realize it until I heard your voice telling him to let me go. So thank you for rushing in to be there for me, even it is a little crazy that you go on a plane with no grantee you would actually find me." I smiled as he stared at me in complete shock.

" You will never cease to amaze me Pigeon." He started the car once more.

" Neither will you." I whispered as we pulled back onto the road, letting the silence fall over us one more. It was comforting to ride in silence. It was the first time in a long time that I was able to bask in the joy of silence, not filled with tension, or the urge to make small talk.

He finally broke the silence when we passed the Welcome to Middleton sign. " Pige, do you mind if I stop and get Maggie? She has been home alone since midnight last night." He said his voice laced with hesitation.

" Not at all." It was all I could muster. I had been trying to figure everything out for the last few hours, and I had done nothing but confuse myself more. I needed to be alone, but Maggie didn't deserve to suffer because my life was a national disaster. I couldn't wrap my head around how I had missed the signs that my husband had been cheating on with his secretary. I couldn't understand why Brandon had flown to Boston to support me. Hell, I still didn't understand why he could come there today and find me, yet all those years ago he couldn't walk into the bar. I wouldn't be in this mess, or this heart broken and unhappy if he hadn't bitched out that night.

From here to forever

I let out the breath I had been holding since I walked into the lawyers office that morning as I climbed out of the car. Relishing in how good it felt to stretch my stiff legs. Brandon was already unlocking the door. Before it was even open Maggie was bounding across the yard ignoring her owner and running full speed at me. I braced myself for her greeting, finding comfort in her wet kissed and cry's of excitement. Brandon hated her in the front yard without leash, so I reached down and grabbed her collar, leading her towards the door.

" I'm just going to feed her and take her for a quick walk around the block. It will take twenty minutes tops." His eyes were filled with concern over my silence. I numbly nodded my head, before curing up in the corner of his couch. I needed to go home so I could curl up in my bed and cry. I sat in the dark unable to hold back all of my tears, and silently began to sob into his pillow.

CHAPTER TWELVE
Brandon

Yet again I am sitting on the floor watching the steady rise and fall of Pigeon's chest. I couldn't bring myself to wake her up so I could take her home. A unusually large part of me was worried that she had actually gone into shock earlier today. There is a very good chance that when she wakes up and today's event sinks in she is going to never speak to me again.

I knew I was taking a serious chance at pissing her off when I got in the car and started driving in the middle of the night. I had tossed and turned for hours before I finally gave up. There was no way I could handle laying in my bed, or pacing my floors, even staying in this town while she was about to go thru hell. I still had no idea what had transpired between her and her husband, I did know that he was the reason she looked like she was knocking on deaths door less then two weeks ago. Just like I knew there was a good chance she was not going to make it out of Boston alive. It was one in the morning when I called Nan, praying that women's need to know every single detail was not going to fail me now.

" Brandon what the hell took you so long? I

wanted to go to sleep hours ago you ass." She yelled into the phone. In all the years I knew Nan she had never been awake pas ten pm. Which meant she has been sitting awake, staring at the phone waiting for me to call her. Sometimes her uncanny sense for knowing what was going to happen freaked me out.

" Sorry Nan, I was really trying to respect her wishes. But damn it she is to stubborn to stop and realize she does need someone there to support her. I can't do it Nan. Okay this has nothing to do with support, I can't lose her to Boston again. I'm going after her. So please tell me that you have the address to that assholes office." I held my breath.

" Like I said it took you long enough. I just text messaged it you Brandon, now go get our girl back. " She had hung up on me before I could marvel in her ability to text message. I was out the door ten minutes later, racing to the airport. I had paced the airport floor impatiently waiting for my flight to board. Pige was going to kill me, she was going to scream, cry, and tell me that she hated me. Yet I couldn't walk away, and I sure as hell wasn't backing down. I had a terrible feeling deep in my gut, and I needed to get to her as fast as possible. For the first time in my life, I didn't have a game plan. A realization that should freak me out. I didn't have time to freak out because the only thing I could think about was not walking into the bar. About letting her walk out of my life. I had to fight this time.

When we finally touched down I was a nervous wreck. In all honesty, I wouldn't be surprised if I was detained and stripped search by the airport police. I had been twitching like I had something to hide for most of the plane ride; I had no carry on, no luggage, not to mention I looked like I was coming down from a very big high.

Pige hadn't seen me sitting by the window in the cafe across the street from the lawyer's office. She took my breath

From here to forever

away as she climbed out of her car. The girl was either looking to win her husband back, or make him regret the day he let her go. That dress was like a second skin hugging ever curve I had worked to put back on her. I left the cafe thirty minutes later, casually walking across the street. I still couldn't understand how she loved it here. The hustle and bustle, all the noise, and not a damn patch of grass in sight. But I finally could understand why she felt like she needed to come here and experience this in order to feel like she lived. I leaned against her passenger's door, waiting for her to walk out of the building. I hadn't purchased a ticket back home, so I was banking on her not being so mad that she left me standing here alone.

I glanced at my watch it was now ten fifteen, and I was really starting to get worried that she was getting eaten alive. Then I saw her. It took everything in my power not to run to her as she pushed thru the door. Tears pouring down her face. She came to a stop searching thru her bag. I watched him fly out the door behind her. I was frozen in shock as he grabbed her arm, jerking her towards him. My hands involuntarily clenched into fists. I was glued to the car if I moved I was going to go to jail for murder.

" Stop" She screamed, and that was it. Something inside of me broke, and I no longer cared if I murdered him right here in the middle of the street.

" I suggest you let her go." I took a step forward praying he listened. He didn't. I closed the distance between Pige's body and mine in a matter of seconds.

" I said let her go Jonathan." Her back was pressed against my chest, I wanted nothing more than to bask in the way her body still fit in mine. The asshole still had not let her go. My pulse was pounding in my ears. I could not even hear him responding to me. I had ever intention of walking away as soon as his hands were off her. But then I blacked out with rage. I have no idea what I said to him. I do know that I finally calmed down enough to pay attention to my surrounds as the words " You'll have to go thru me, and that's not a fight I'm going to lose." Left my mouth. I was nose to nose with the bastard that thought he could man handle my girl. Pigeon was three steps behind me. I stepped back continuing to shield her body with mine, I didn't start to relax until I had her behind the locked passengers door of her car. I reached the drivers door and stared down Jonathan, I didn't open my door until he turned his back and walked away. I help my breath terrified of how mad Pige was going to be. Not only had I ignored her wishes. But also I had just threatened her soon to be ex-husband, and essentially marked Pige as my territory. I opened the door and climbed, and getting ready to have my ass chewed out.

    The chewing out hadn't happened, and neither did an explanation as to what happened, or why Jonathan was forcefully grabbing her in the middle of the street. Ironically enough the only thing I was shocked about was the lack of screaming on the car ride home. Pige hadn't shared anything about what had happened in her marriage, unless you count her first night home when she was drunk.

    Maggie curled herself into a ball next to me. I lay down with my head on her back and decided if I could just rest my eyes for a minute or two, then I would take her home. Just so I could finally get some sleep. After being away awake for forty hours, it was heaven letting my eyes rest, even if I was ridiculously uncomfortable.

CHAPTER THIRTEEN
Elizabeth

I woke up sometime during the night, with a still neck. As well as freezing cold. I quickly got my bearings. There on the floor just a few feet from the couch lay Brandon and Maggie. Both of them sound asleep. I slipped off my heels and tiptoed out of the living room. On the table by the front door was my cell phone and car keys. I put my car in neutral and coasted down his driveway. Not giving it any gas until I was on the road. I made it home in record time. Not bothering to turn the car off I sprinted to the front door. Five minutes later I was back in the car with two duffle bags shoved in the truck, holding my breath. I couldn't really breath until I was out of town and back on the highway.

I know what you are thinking. What kind of stupid woman I am to go running back to the husband that cheated on her? The husband who couldn't handle the fact that my chances of having children were slim to none. The husband who hated that I was an author, hated the book tours, hated the fans who recognized me in the grocery store. The husband who has never once so much as read one word out of any of my five published books. How could I run back to the prick that made sure he got one last lay before he casually announced he wanted a divorce? Well your right I would be a stupid ass. Which is exactly why I am not going back to him. I am however running the hell away., and fast.

    Yes, you read that right I am running away. Away from Brandon and the feelings I don't want to have for him. Away from my over bearing grandmother who has hijacked my life because she loves me and wants to see me happy. Even though she has no idea how to do that. I am running away from my best friend who tells me everything I don't want to hear, because at the end of the day it's actually the truth. I am running away from her family, and her happy marriage, because I am not a good friend right now. I am jealous and starting to resent her for having everything I want and can't have. Most of all I am running away so I can have ten minutes of silence to sort out the current state of my life. I made my way through the Leigh High valley tunnel. Thanking god I had never told anyone about the little two-bedroom house that sits on a lake in the middle of ten acres. Nestled in the Pocono mountains. The house that only get cell reception when you stand out side on the very end of the dock.

    It was also the only place in the world where I could find comfort on my own. It wasn't cluttered with memories, or history. I was the only person who had ever been there. I had every intention of hiding away for the next few days, and not speaking to anyone until I had a better grasp on my sanity. While I was here I needed desperately to figure out what my next novel was going to be about. My agent had been breathing down my neck for the last month, the publisher is getting anxious, and my fans are becoming impatient. I wanted to write I honestly did. I just couldn't find a way to put the words onto paper. Hell I didn't even know what words to put on the paper. My life was a mess. If I didn't figure out a way to sort that out, there was no way in hell I was going help my fictional characters get their happy ever after. I pulled onto the gravel driveway of the place that had become my sanctuary over the years. I have hidden out here more times than I can count. Book tours that were only scheduled for a week turned into two so I could find some silence and peace without revealing where I was. Yeah I lied to Jonathan, but seriously come the hell on, the man has been screwing someone else. Someone who announced at my dinner table three months ago that she was expecting.

That mother humper. How did I not put two and two together yesterday and get three? That little slut bag truly was giving him everything I couldn't. Right now I should be seeing red, and I seriously want to, I do. I'm sure you are like oh no she didn't. But in all honesty I'm to damn tired to be mad. I haven't truly felt rested in forever. I have every intention of walking into this house, filling up the antique claw tub with my expensive bath salts and oils, and soaking until my entire body looks like a prune. Then I am going to climb into bed, pull the black out shades down, and just sleep until my body is rested. My phone started vibrating in the cup holder as I turned the car off. I picked it up six text messages from Brandon.

4:01 AM. Pige did u go home did u get home ok and u ok??????

6:17 AM Where are u? I just drove by ur house to make sure u got there ok, and ur car is gone what's going on P?

8:00 AM Pige seriously where are you Nan and Madison said they haven't heard from u since u got to Boston

8:05 AM Nan says you better call her and let her know that u are alive.

8:15 AM God Damn it Pige where the hell are u. Nan is pissed, and I am seriously getting worried.

8:33 Elizabeth Breeze Cole this is your grandmother. Your ass better be dead in a god damn gutter right now if it's not I am going to put it there myself.

I sighed of course he would wake up and realize I was gone. Just like he had to be a damn stalker and drive past my house at six in the morning to make sure I was there. I knew without a doubt that he had Nan out of bed by 6:30. By now Madison was pacing Nan's kitchen floor while Nan ranted and raved, and Brandon cursed me under his breath. I hit reply.

8:35 AM I am fine. I need to take some time for me. I have gone to my sanctuary. Little to no cell reception, will be back when I have some clarity, and rest. You can all be pissed, but I am to exhaust to care. Sorry for worrying you.

I hit send and turned my phone off. I climbed out of the car, and walked into the house, and promptly locked the door, before stumbling down the hall to the bed. The bath can wait, my body had finally put her foot down, and sleep was calling my name. My eyes closed as I tried to ignore the nagging thought that I missed Brandon's whimpering in his sleep.

CHAPTER FOURTEEN
Elizabeth

I finally turned my phone back on two days ago. Only long enough to check my e-mails. That had been the plan before I discovered fifty two-text message, two hundred and thirty seven e-mails, and my voicemail box full. I quickly sent off an e-mail to my agent and editor letting them know I was hiding out in my mountain retreat. They both knew there was no cell reception, and no internet. They also would both assume that meant I was working on something book related.

I had been there five days at that point in time, and had not done a single thing, but sleep, soak in the tub, and try to figure out what my next move was. I read thru my other e-ails and texts while sitting on the edge of the dock. Uncrossing my legs while slipping off my shoes and dipping my feet into the pond. I wasn't surprised to discover Nan was the only person who hadn't called. Which meant the text message she sent from Brandon's phone days ago had ben sent to keep face with frick and frack, or Brandon and Madison. Of course, she had to appear mad, so she wouldn't let on that she knew damn right well where I was. Nothing could ever be sacred or kept a secret when she was your grandmother. I honestly would bet that she knew I bought the house before I even made settlement on it. I shouldn't have been surprised, in all honesty.

I looked back down at my phone, scrolling thru my contacts for the fiftieth time. I closed my eyes, lying back on the dock. In a moment of clarity. I suddenly knew exactly what I needed to do, after being cooped up alone for seven day I was ready to close some chapters of my life, so I could explore some others.

1:52pm I think we need to talk, I'm at my sanctuary in the Poconos how soon can you be here?

1:53pm I am already on my way. See u soon.

I let out the breath I had been holding, trying to push down my self-doubt as I made my way into my house. Which clearly is not as much of a secret as I once wished it was. I sat down on the arondeck chair in the yard waiting for him to arrive so we could close this chapter once and for all.

CHAPTER FIFTEEN
Brandon

It has been a week since Pige packed up and ran away in the middle of the night. While she was off getting her clarity and rest, I was miserable. At least the last time she left she had said goodbye. She couldn't even say that this time. Nope, poof she was gone. One simple text that basically said I'm a pussy and ran away. To make everything worse her asshole husband has been having flowers delivered to her house everyday three god damn times a day. The house that I am busy trying to finish, because it is killing me to be in it knowing that she is gone. The sooner I get it done, the sooner the daily reminder can stop. I walked thru her kitchen, trying to call her for the five hundredth time in the past two days.

" You have reached the voicemail of" the automated voice chimed in my ear. Right to voicemail of course. Just like the last four hundred and ninety nine times. I took one look at the counter filled with vases of roses. She hated roses, and he was married to her for the love of god. How could he not know she hated roses? I swiped my arm down the counter in a flurry of rage shattering twenty vases onto the floor.

" You know she has to come back sooner or later?" Nan's voice startled me.

" Sorry Nan I will clean this up I promise." I weakly smiled at her.

" Do you really think I give a shit? I am half tempted to send them back to that bastard." She pulled out a chair and pointed for me to sit. " I know that none of us have ever talked about what happened that night all those years ago. But I think it's time I explained a few things to you. Elizabeth and I did talk. We had a very long talk in the days that followed. Not because I was mad, or upset with either of you. You guys were teenagers doing what teenagers do. She was on the pill it wasn't like you weren't being careful. We talked because she needed it, and I was the only one she knew would completely understand. Brandon what happened that night made you both grow up. It made you both wonder what would have happened if it had been a normal pregnancy, and if she hadn't miscarried. I know it weighed heavy on your mind, but it changed her." She paused taking a deep breath.

" I know it changed her, it also ruined her marriage." I slammed my fist down on the table.

" Brandon James, check your temper at the door. You will sit there quietly and listen to what I have to say damn it. I have held this in for a very long time. Just like I have watch the two of you dance around your feeling for each other for year. Do we understand each other?" I had forgotten until this awful moment just how terrifying Nan could be. She was not a woman you ever wanted pissed off at you.

" Yes ma'am." I involuntarily nodded my head as I confirmed I would sit quietly until she was done.

" Brandon when she lost the baby she didn't know she was having, as well as basically lost the ability to become pregnant, she decided she needed to find something else to full fill her. She needed something she could pour herself into, and a career that could become her baby. That night was also the night she decided she was going to go to college in Boston. You know as well as I do she always loved to read and write. But it wasn't until she got to school that she decided she wanted to be a writer. Leaving for Boston was the hardest thing she has ever done. I can grantee it was harder than facing that prick the other day, it was harder than moving back here, hell it's harder than the miscarriage. It was so hard because she knew she was walking away from you. I don't know how much you know about her mama. But I'm going to bring you up to speed. Her mother got knocked up at twenty, she had no clue who the father was, and didn't want a child. I talked her out of having an abortion. We agreed we would raise her together. Her mama dropped out of school, moved back home and gave birth to Izzy. She also skipped out of the hospital five hours after giving birth. That is how I ended up raising my granddaughter. I never lied to her about her mother. But that night when the two of you lost the baby, Izzy became terrified that she was going to become her mother. She was so afraid that both of your futures almost went down the drain. She was afraid to leave you to go to Boston because she didn't want to skip out on you like her mother did. That my dear boy is how I know she will be back. She didn't say goodbye this time, she won't let herself become her mother. You know her mama has tried to have a relationship with her a few times. But by the time she was ten Izzy wouldn't agree to meet her anymore. There are only so many broken promises and disappearing acts in the middle of the night one person can take before they throw in the towel. It didn't help her mama started drinking bad after she was born." Nan stood up and walked to the sink. Giving it all a moment to sink in.

" Nan she did leave without saying goodbye. She woke up on my couch, snuck out of the house drove home and then just left." I understand the point she is trying to make. But she failed. Pige left, she packed up, and she left without a goodbye.

" Brandon she answered our text messages, and she told us where she was. She is coming back trust me." Nan sighed, looking extremely frustrated with me.

" Yeah, she told us she was at her sanctuary. That didn't exactly tell us where she was." I could hear my temper slipping back into my voice.

" I know where she is, and I will gladly tell you as soon as you and I have another little talk, about this god forsaken dance the two of you have been doing since kindergarten." She sat back down, holding up her hand when I tried to speak. " You are both stubborn, pig headed, idiots, who ignore their feelings, and let their brains and self doubts continue to rule your lives. Instead of listening to your hearts. I get it she left and went to Boston to go to school. That was a minor hill in your relationship, and rather then work thru it you both just walked the hell away. Don't even try to tell me you didn't. You went to Boston, stood outside of the bar you were supposed to meet her in, and then walked the hell away. You were no better then she was a week ago when she didn't tell you what was going on. You know she meet Jonathan that night. She put off going out with him for weeks, holding out hope that you would call and tell her that you loved her. You never did Brandon. You walked away without a goodbye. She waited two months before she finally gave up and went on a date with that prick. So it's finally time to spill it why didn't you go into the bar that night?" She let the question hang in the air, not rushing my answer, just sitting with her chin resting in her hands.

" I..." My voice trailed off. " I just couldn't bring myself to walk in the door." I started again, once again finding myself at a loss for words. I closed my eyes, remembering standing on the busy street, shivering against the chill in the air. She had been sitting with her back to the door at a table filled with people I assumed she went to school with. I reached for the door handle as she threw her head back laughing. I stepped back from the door and watched her from the shadows. It wasn't until she turned to look for me that I finally walked away.

" Nan, I couldn't walk into the bar because I didn't fit into her new life. I was just some country boy with no idea about how the world worked, or who I was. It was like over night she had found her place in the world. I knew that if I walked thru that door I was only going to hold her back. So yeah, I may not have said goodbye. But I loved the girl to damn much, there was no way I could actually say goodbye to her when it was the last thing in the world I wanted." I had never tried to put words to why I left her waiting. There were no words to truly describe why I did it. It took a awful long time before I could even justify it to myself. In a way, I guess I selflessly walked away and made myself miserable, so she could follow her dreams and find her happiness without being held back.

" Have you figured out who you are, or where you belong yet?" Nan interrupted me thoughts, jerking me back into the present.

I shrugged my shoulders. Do I know who I am, or where I belong? I let my head fall forward, resting on the table. " I am the person who took over the family business. So by default here in Middleton is where I belong." Nan just sat staring at me slowly nodding her head. I stood up and walked out of the kitchen. I paused when I reached the front door, the nob half turned in my hand. I wasn't just some handy man who ran his daddy's business damn it. I had worked my ass off to be more. I turned fully intending to march back out to the kitchen.

" I am going to ask you again." She was leaning against the wall ten feet behind me. " Do you know who you are, what you want and where you belong?"

" Damn it Nan, you already know I have two different college degrees, my own business, house, and calm stable life. That's who I am. But it's not what I want. I want Pige, she is who I have always wanted, who I will always want. I am not going to rest until she gives me another chance, I belong where she is. Now are you going to tell me where my girl is?" I took a step towards her, placed my hands on my hips, just as her face broke out in a wide smile.

" Amen, took you long enough. I would have told you were she was days ago. But you were still busy dancing your I don't love her dance. She is going to be pissed that you are there, and accuse you of stalking her. She thinks no one knows were the house is. Just so happens I was casually seeing the father of the real estate agent that sold it to her." She reached out and dropped a piece of paper into my hand. "Boy what the hell are you still standing here for? Go bring your girl home. I took another step away from the door, closing the distance between Nan and I. I wrapped my arms around her pulling her into a fierce hug.

" Thank you Nan." I pressed a kiss onto the top of her head. I raced to the car, needing to get to Pige as fast as possible.

CHAPTER SIXTEEN
Brandon

Any other time I would leisurely driving the speed limit. Rolling down the windows to let the fresh mountain air assault me. I would be taking in the deep rolling mountain ranges covered in a wide array of green, enjoying the refreshingness of there not being any houses in sight. Today I was flying down the highway, desperate to get to Pige. I needed to explain, to fix things. I needed to tell the damn girl that I loved her. It had taken me long enough to admit it to myself, I couldn't wait a minute longer to tell her. Turning into her drive way the gravel flying under my tires. I slammed on the brakes as I reached her car. My breath hitched in my throat. Beside her car sat a black convertible. I put the car in reverse. Clearly she wasn't sitting up here alone.

" You can't do this again." I yelled at myself, before slamming the car in park and jumping out. I couldn't let my fear win this time. I had lost her once because I hadn't been willing to fight. I had to at least fight this time. If she didn't want me in her life fine. But I wasn't going down without a fight. I took the front steps two at a time. I stopped at the front door, unable to knock. Pige's voice seeping out stopped me in my tracks. I couldn't make out what she was saying, but I could hear the panic and anger in her voice. My adrenalin kicked into over drive. I threw open the door, and my worse fears were confirmed.

    Her back was to me as she was caught in an intimate embrace. Her leg was hitched up around his hip, her arms were fisted in his shirt, and Jonathan had his hand on her thigh pulling her leg tighter to him as they made up. Her voice hadn't been angry clearly it had been full of passion. I should just turn and walk away, pretend like I had never come. Yet I couldn't seem to hold back the words that were bubbling up in my chest.

    " Nan will be so happy to hear that you alive Pigeon, and even happier to hear that you weren't up here wallowing in pity. No, you were making up with the prick that cheated on you, suppressed you creativity, and truly has no idea who the hell you are. To think I came here to fight for you. Clearly I am a dollar short and a lifetime to late." I screamed, Jonathan's smug smile taunting me.

    " Brandon wait, please." She cried as tears escaped her lashes. I turned not wanting her to see my heart breaking and fled. I sprinted to the car and threw it in reverse. I couldn't get the hell out of there fast enough. I glanced in my rearview mirror, which was a colossal mistake. There Pige stood, tears streaming down her face, and Jonathan on the front porch arms crossed looking like a man who had just won the lottery. Clearly she wouldn't be staying in Middleton. Thankfully I already knew Nan would understand if I delayed finishing the project until she was gone. The scenery I had wished I could enjoy on the ride up was now nothing but a blur, as I sped away from the girl I loved, and the life shattering pain she had just inflicted on me. The sooner I could get home the better. A cold six pack and a few days alone is all it will take to lock everything back up again. Where it belong, where it should have stayed hidden.

From here to forever

CHAPTER SEVENTEEN
Elizabeth

I could not believe what I was hearing. Brandon was here, standing in my house at the worst possible moment. I had asked Jonathan here so we could put this all to rest. After I listened to his twenty voice-mails, read his fifty text messages, and scrolled thru the seventy-five e-mails I knew I had to see him. It would be easier if we did it face to face. I needed answers, and he needed to understand there was no way in hell I was ever going to take him back. Look I know most people wouldn't invite their soon to be ex husband to the place that is supposed to be their sanctuary. But I did. Mostly because for eight years he had been the person I shared my life with, and if I was going to get closure I feel like it needs to be face to face. However, hindsight is twenty twenty.

I stood in the driveway watching Brandon drive away. I should get in my car and flag him down, make him listen, but I didn't I turned around and snapped.

" What the hell is your problem? I asked you here so we could work out final details so I could get closure, so we could both walk away not hating each other. What the hell did you think was going to happen huh? You got your secretary pregnant, congrats on that I guess asshole. You have more than likely moved her into my house already too right? Turned the office into a nursery? You have everything you ever wanted in life. So what the hell possessed to sexually assault me. You can't even say you didn't for the love of god I kneed you in the balls before you grabbed my leg and wrapped it around your waist. You are a real asshole you know that? Brandon was right you are nothing but a douche bag. Get the hell out of my house before I call the police and have you arrested." I held the door open waiting for him to leave.

" Izzy, I don't love her I love you. I just had to do the noble thing you know she having my kid." He paused reaching his hand out towards my face.

" You lay one more finger on my and I swear to go I am going cut your dick off. Get out so I can try to make things right with Brandon." I stood taping my foot waiting for Jonathan to move.

" The same Brandon that stood you up all those years ago? To think he finally found the balls to walk thru the door, only to discover that once again he was too late." He laughed as he walked past me, shoving his shoulder into me on his way by. I didn't wait for him to reach the steps before I slammed the door. I know for a fact it literally hit him in the ass on his way out. I grabbed my cell phone and sprinted to the dock. For the first time, I hated the lack of cell service. I needed to stop him, and I didn't have another five minutes to waste running to the dock. As soon as I had one bar I was dialing his number praying that he would pick up.

" Hey guys its Brandon you know what to do." His voicemail chimed in my ear.

" Brandon, is Iz please call me I swear it's not what it looked like. I didn't want him to kiss me I was trying to get him off me. Please please call me." I hung up feeling the tears slip over my lashes. Maybe he was just in the tunnel that ran thru the mountain. No one ever got cell reception when they went thru there. I paced back and forth waiting for him to call me back. I looked at the screen only to discover that five minutes had passed. I hit send on his number; I no longer cared if it had only been five minutes.

" Hey guys." I hung up and started pacing again. I wasn't going inside until he answered. I could feel it in the pit of my stomach the longer it took for him to call me back, the worse the feeling got. Something was wrong, tremendously wrong. I was trapped at the edge of the dock, unable to leave for fear of missing his call, and desperately needing to get in my car and drive until I was home and on his doorstep.

Once again I looked at my cell phone for the hundredth time. It had been five hours since he sped out of my driveway. My cell phone rang, causing me to jump with the jarring ring breaking thru the deafening silence.

" Hello Brandon, I swear it wasn't what it looked like. Please don't hang up, please, please I need you to listen to me." I was sobbing uncontrollably.

" Elizabeth, it isn't Brandon. Hun are you sitting down?" Nan's voice froze my sobs, the breath in my chest, and my heart stopped beating.

" What is wrong? Why do I need to be sitting down?" I whispered as a shiver of fear shook my body.

" Izzy, it's Brandon, you need to come home." Her voice broke as I crumbled to the ground. Everything moved in slow motion, and I swear I actually heard my world cracking around me.

" Nan what is wrong, what is wrong with Brandon?" I forced the words out.

" He was in a car accident. Izzy I don't know how to tell you this. He was just rushed into surgery, but they aren't sure he is going to make it. You need to come home sweetie." Her voice finally broke, and she quietly sobbed into the receiver.

" I'm on my way." I hung up, pulling myself up onto my knees. I crossed myself like I had seen Nan do a million times, and for the first time in years I prayed.

" Dear God, I know I don't talk to you that much, I never go to church, and I break a lot of commandments, but I need you. I really, really need you right now. I didn't pray to you when my husband left me. I have never really asked you for anything before. But I need a big one now. God you can't take Brandon, you just can't take him from me. I need him, and it has taken me forever to realize it. Please god I can't lose him again, I can't lose him before we really have a chance at loving each other. Please just let him hang on until I can tell him that I love him, that I have loved him since the minute I met him when he pulled my pigtails on the first day of kindergarten. Please I promise I will never ask you for anything again." I was sobbing staring at the sky on my knees begging with no shame. I stood up sprinting to the house. Key, laptop, phone were all I grabbed nothing else was important. I needed to get to Brandon to the hospital. I just needed him to hang on long enough for me to hold his hand one last time.

I was flying down the highway minutes later. I looked at my speedometer as I turned onto the turnpike. I was going over one hundred and ten, and the only way I was stopping was if my tires were shot out. God must have sent an angel to ride on my shoulder home because the turnpike was damn near empty, and for once there wasn't a cop in sight.

I somehow got myself under control when I pulled into the hospital parking lot. I sprinted thru the doors, taking the stairs to the third floor where Brandon currently was, three at a time. I pushed open the doors, and my heart dropped. Half the town was sitting in the waiting room. Nan was talking quietly in the corner with Brandon's mother and the priest. Madison was huddled in her husbands lap crying. Nan walked towards me, arms opening for a hug.

" Where is he, please I need to see him." The tears started to fall again as his mother walked towards me. I opened my arms and let her and Nan hold me close to them.

" Of course you can sweetie, his room is down that hall third door on the left. I have already cleared it with the nurse. But I should warn you he is in bad shape." His mother voice broke a sob racking her body. I pulled her tighter to me, suddenly numb. " His truck it was… it was t-boned by a tractor trailer on the drivers side. They want to take him in to surgery soon they were waiting for some cat scans and MRI's to come back. You should go see him. We will have time to talk soon." His mother took my arm and led me down the hallway. Giving me a gentle push when we reached his door. I squeezed her hand before opening the door.

I let out a gasp as I pulled back the curtain. This had to be a sick joke. That wasn't my Brandon lying in that bed. His face was unrecognizable. A gash ran from the corner of his eye diagonally down his face stopping at his jaw. Both of his eyes were bruising and almost swollen shut. He had a tube down his throat as well as a breathing tube in his nose. The steady hum and beeping were the only indication that he was alive. I stood next to his bed terrified that touching him would somehow hurt him, or screw up a monitor. Both of his hands had IV's in them; I slid mine into his sinking down to my knees for the second time today.

" Brandon, it's Pige. I am so sorry, about everything. About what happened when we were younger, about not fighting for you when we were eighteen, about running away a week ago, and most of all for not stopping you today. I was closing the Jonathan chapter today. You actually walked in thirty seconds after I kneed him in the balls. I love you. I have always loved you. Damn it you have to pull thru, you have to be okay because it has taken me almost twenty-five years to admit that I can't live without you. You are my happily ever after. I have spent years searching for what would truly make me happy in life, and I had it all along. It was you. I need you to fight. Please please fight because I need more time with you. I need forever, I need you to drive me insane, push my buttons, and to understand me better than anyone else. Damn it you can't leave me. You have to fight, you can't die without telling me why you have called me Pige since day one in our relationship." My head rested on the edge of his bed, tears streaming down my face as I choked out the last sentence. I knew if he woke up right now, he would give me shit for begging.

" Come on now Pige begging really? You are above that. "He would tease, reaching down a hand to help me to my feet.

" You are worth begging for." I whispered as I stood up. I leaned over pressing my lips to his lips. " Fight for me Brandon, please fight." A tear rolled off my check and onto his.

" Miss I am sorry we will be taking him in just a moment, we have waited as long as we could." I nodded my head, turning back to Brandon one last time.

" I loved you yesterday, I love you still, I have never stopped, and I never will. I love you Brandon." I said into his lips, kissing him one last time. I stood back watching them wheel him out of the room. Following into the hallway, unable to take my eyes off of him. I didn't breath until he was out of sight. As the doors closed behind them I felt my knees begin to buckle, a sob broke thru my lips just as I was swept off my feet.

" I gotcha Iz." Jim whispered into my hair. I felt him set me down, and someone else take my hand. Nan, Madison, and Lily Brandon's mom's voices floated around me. Nothing they said made sense. I just sat staring at the clock on the wall, watching the seconds tick by.

CHAPTER EIGHTEEN
Elizabeth

I must have drifted off to sleep at some point in time. I felt my self being shaken awake. I jumped to my feet panic crushing my chest.

" He is out of surgery dear." He mother squeezed my hand.

" How, how is he?" My voice shook, terrified of what the answer could be.

" He is stable, they have relieved the pressure on his brain. One of his lungs collapsed during surgery, and his heart stopped twice. But right now he is stable." I felt her squeeze my hand, waiting for my response. I couldn't bring myself to say anything.

" Sweetie, why don't we take you to your house? You can get a little sleep maybe eat something." Madison was talking to me. I couldn't understand why she thought I would leave. I wasn't leaving until Brandon did. I was starting to feel like I was in the twilight zone. Nothing anyone said made any sense.

" I'm not leaving Madison. Mama L can I see him?" My voice sounded robotic echoing in my ears.

" Yes darling, of course you can." She stared at me in confusion.

" Great, I am just going to run to the restroom quickly." I turned walking briskly down the hall. I splashed water on my face trying to snap myself out of it. I think there is only so much stress and worry one person can take before they snap. Tonight I think I have reached mine. I wonder if I can figure out the signs of shock without getting myself admitted to the hospital. I threw another hand full of water on my face as the door open.

" Izzy are you okay?" Madison closed the door, coming to stand beside me. I turned to look at her, plastering a smile across my face.

" Yes I am." My voice trailed off. She stood there with her arm resting on the tampon dispenser. I could feel myself go pale. My vision began to fade as I collapsed to the floor.

" Izzy." Madison shrieked reaching out for me. Her voice sounded so far away. This could not be happening. " Izzy, god damn it talk to me before I get a doctor." She was shaking my shoulders. I wonder if she knew her face was terribly out of focus.

" I'm late." I mumbled in a hushed voice.

" Your late? Late for what? Sweetie I am really worried about you. I think maybe you should go home with me or Nan tonight." She was squeezing my hand again, I could feel her. Yet she still seemed so far away.

" I am late, seven days late." My vision began to focus. Madison slowly went from blurry to clear. Her eyes wide, her mouth forming an O and she was now rumpled in front of me.

"Jonathans?" She asked.

" No, not his. I had my period shortly after he left me." I watched her face glass over with confusion.

" It's not? I can't be? Is it? Did you?" I watched her try to wrap her head around the concept. Even she couldn't speak the truth out loud.

" Yes, it's Brandon's." The tears started to fall, again.

" You slut. How could you not tell me you two screwed? You hussy. Iz, I'm guessing you haven't taken a test yet right?" Her hand came to rest on top of mine. Both of us holding my stomach. I shook my head no.

" It was the night we watched Guy's and Dolls. That was a month ago." I whispered as the memory washed back over me.

He had gently pulled the quilt down over me, placing a kiss on my forehead. I opened my eyes throwing caution to the wind. I slid up his body capturing his lips with mine. His teeth gently tugged on my lip, as his hand splayed across my back pulling me closer to him. My fingers had tangled in his hair tugging him closer to me. I had pulled back intending to stop it. But the look of lust in his eyes had me ripping my clothes off. His mouth found my breast tugging gently on my nipple as a low moan escaped my lips.

"God you are beautiful." He whispered into my neck as he flipped me onto my back, coming to rest on his knees between my legs. I reached for his pants desperate to have them off him. I had forgotten how incredible Brandon feels until he was pushing himself into me. We hadn't stopped to consider consequences. Instead I grabbed his ass pulling him deeper into me. Lost completely in the moment getting lost in how shocking it felt to be wanted again. I let myself scum to the ecstasy, reveling in how well he filled me, how he fit like a glove.

" You go in and see Brandon. I am going to send Jim home. Give me your keys, and I will be back in less then twenty minutes." Madison snapped me back to reality.

" We didn't use a condom, and I'm not on the pill. But holy shit it was mind blowing." I mumbled as a blush crept up my neck, just thinking about the two other times I had let him have his way with me that night.

" No, shit Sherlock. I kind of assumed as much." She pulled me to my feet. I slide my car keys into her hand as we left the bathroom.

" Everything okay darling." Brandon's mother was at my side.

From here to forever

" Yes, I'm just going to go back to see Brandon. I will probably stay with him the rest of the night if that is okay?" I glanced at the clock behind me it was after midnight, and his mother looked exhausted.

" Are you sure you don't mind." She stifled a yawn.

" Lily I have no intentions of leaving until he wakes up. Why don't you go get some sleep? I will call you if anything changes. " I smiled, as a quick look of relief flashed across her face.

" Thank you." She pressed her lips to my check pulling me into a quick hug before she walked away. Nan squeezed my hand before climbing onto the elevator. There were no words needed between Nan and I. She knew there was nothing that she could say to comfort me or get me to leave. I glanced around the waiting room as the elevator doors closed. The crowd was gone leaving just me standing alone. I made my way back to Brandon's room. Closing the door behind me. I drug the chair across the room and sat down once again taking his hand into mine.

" Hey you, it me." I brushed my lips against his knuckles. " Surgery went well. Now all you need to do is rest so your body can heal. Brandon, please don't stop fighting." I let the tears fall freely in the dark room. I laid my head on his bed, needing to be as close to him as possible. I heard the door open after what seemed like a lifetime.

" I got them." Madison hissed.

" Why are you whispering?" I hissed back.

" I don't want to get his hopes up. Get in his bathroom now." She tugged on my arm. I stood up.

" Brandon I'll be right back." I kissed him on his check before following Madison into the bathroom. .

" Here pee on these. " She shoved me towards the toilet handing me three sticks.

" All of them?"

" Yes all of them now hurry up." She turned on the water, and began tapping her foot. We stood watching our phones waiting for three minutes to pass. In all honesty, the suspense is enough to drive you insane. I honestly think they should make an instant results pregnancy test. That way when it comes up pregnant, and you shit yourself you are already on the toilet. We watched as each one slowly revealed a plus sign. I reached for Madison as my knees gave out again.

"I'm, I'm I'm," my voice trailed off.

" Having a baby sweetie." Madison was cupping my face. Her own face was streaked with tears. The irony of this situation was more then I could handle. My first pregnancy had resulted in the belief that I couldn't have children. I had spent six years trying to get pregnant with my ex, trying being the key word. Now by some sick twist of fate I am pregnant by the exact person who knocked me up the first time. Oh yeah and that person is laying in a hospital bed, and no one knows if he is ever going to wake up again. I lay down letting the chilly tile ground me.

This was one of those moments where I loved my best friend more than I could ever explain. She lay down face me, taking both of my hands in hers. We lay on our sides not speaking for a few minutes.

" He is going to wake up. He loves you to damn much to leave you. Besides if loving you wasn't enough of a reason to fight, this will be." She pressed her hand to my belly once more.

" Thank you." I climbed to my feet and walked out of the bathroom. " Bran, I need you to hurry up and heal. I need you to open your goddamn eyes. Brandon we are having a baby, I am pregnant. I know I screwed up, and I know that this is all my fault. I will never forgive myself if you never wake up. If you can't forgive me I will understand, but please don't stop fighting for your child." I felt Madison's hand on my shoulder.

From here to forever

" I love you both." She squeezed my shoulder once and then was gone. I lay my head down on the bed, letting sleep over take me.

CHAPTER NINETEEN
Elizabeth

It had been four weeks since Brandon's accident. After the first three days, the hospital staff quickly learned that I truly had no plans of leaving. They had been courteous enough to bring me in a recliner, as well give me access to the staff locker room so I could clean up without needing to go home. Madison and Nan were still coming by once a day to check on me. They had brought me clothes, and toiletries, replacing them when I ran out. Brandon was stable, the swelling in his brain had gone down, he was breathing on his own. His brain activity looked good as well. Yet he still hadn't opened his eyes, spoken, or moved on his own. I have spent every minute willing him to move a finger, or open his eyes. Any sign that he was going to recover would do.

    The doctors had been abundantly clear that there was a chance he would never wake up. If I heard the brain is a funny thing, one more time I was going to scream. The door opened behind me the familiar sound of medical equipment being rolled in snapped me out of my day dream. I glanced at the clock on the wall, it was to early for the daily brain activity test on Brandon.

    " Ms. Cole, My name is Dr. Anderson." A thin blond stood in

front of me her hand extended. I reached out and shook it, trying to remember who she was. " I will be your **OBGYN** during this pregnancy. Your friend Madison approached me last week and explained the situation. I also had your previous medical records pulled. I understand that you were previously advised that your chances of becoming pregnant were basically non-existent. With that in mind, I would like to do an ultrasound, and briefly check you over today to make sure that everything is ok?" She stood staring at me, waiting for my response.

" Can we do it here? I know you probably think I am crazy, but I feel like even though he isn't awake he needs to be here for this. That maybe, just maybe it would help. " I was crying again. Between the throw up and crying over nothing at all I was getting mighty tired of my hormone. She crouched down in front of me and wrapped her arms around me.

" Shh, I don't think you are crazy, in fact I think that is one of the most beautiful things I have ever heard." She pulled back, her eyes misting over with tears. She stood up and took Brandon's hand in hers. " Well Brandon, what do you say we start this appointment? Are you ready to hear you child's heart beat?" She squeezed his hand once more before turning back to me.

" Thank you." I whispered wiping the new round of tears from my eyes. She turned and took both my hands in hers squeezing them.

" It is my pleasure. I am going to need to put the recliner back, and then I am going to ask that you lay down and pull up your shirt ok." She said as she reclined the chair as far back as it would go. I lay down after she stepped aside pulling up my shirt. I reached over and laced my finger thru Brandon's.

" Are you both ready?" She asked. I could hug this remarkable woman in front of me. She was the first person who actually spoke to Brandon like he was awake, like he was still him. She understood that above all else, this is what I needed to keep it together right now. I looked over at Brandon and squeezed his hand, still hoping that he would squeeze it back.

" Yes we are." I turned my face back towards hers.

" This is going to be cold." She plugged in the portable ultrasound machine, before squirting jelly onto my stomach. I turned to watch the monitor, and the tears once again began to flow freely. " That right there, is your baby." She pointed to the monitor, where a tiny little sack lay with a steady pulse thumping in the middle. " That is your baby's heart." Her finger sat just under the pulse, and I began to sob.

" Can we hear it?" I choked out.

"Yes of course you can. Let me just take a photo for the two of you." She smiled down at me. I reached over and squeezed Brandon's hand again.

" That's out little peanut Bran." I whispered.

" Oh my god." I heard in unison from the door. My eyes flew open wide I looked around the doctor, and there stood Nan and Lily. They held each other tears streaming down their faces.

" Ladies I am sorry I will have to ask that you wait out side." Dr. Anderson turned suddenly fiercely protective.

" No, no it's okay that is my grandmother and his mother. I hadn't told them yet. I didn't want to get your hopes up. Please stay." My eyes were begging them to forgive me for keeping it a secret. I didn't have to ask them twice. Nan came to my left side taking my hand in hers. While Lilly came and sat gingerly on the edge of Brandon's bed, laying her hand on top of our interlocked hands. I blinked thru my tears as Madison's voice filled the room.

" Damn it, I tried to wait outside. But that is my god child in there. No, I am not giving you a choice. I sat on that bathroom floor in there with you the night you found out. I have been here every day making sure you eat and take you vitamins. I kept a secret from Nan, and set up this appointment. Damn it bitch I am coming in to, or I am going to throw the fit of a century." She stamped her foot, resting her hands on her hips. I took my hands back and held them out to her. That was all she needed before she was pulling me to her, in a fierce hug.

" Maddie, thank you for making sure this child is okay, when I couldn't remember how to take care of myself. There is no one else in the world I would want to take care of him or her if something happened to us. I reached back over squeezing Brandon's hand. We would like to ask you to formally be its godmother. We would also like to ask that the three of you raise this child like it is your own if anything should happen to us. I have recently learned just how fragile life is, and if I had to leave this child to anyone in this world it would be the three of you." I looked at each face in the room, finding that each of them where nodding, with tears streaming down their faces. Dr. Anderson discreetly wiped the tears that were rolling down her cheek.

" Okay ladies, since you all showed up a little late, let me show you the baby." Lily's hand once again gripped our intertwined hands. While Nan and Madison gripped my left hand. Three gasps escaped at the same time. I couldn't tear my eyes away from the screen. " Now if you are already I would like to let you all hear the heart beat. She picked up five ultrasound pictures passing one to each of us. She walked around Brandon's bed with the last one in her hands. She lay it gently in his free hand, before coming back to me. She placed a new monitor on my almost unnoticeable baby bump.

A steady thumping filled the silent room. As I tried to wrap my head around how beautiful it sounded a felt a tiny squeeze in my right hand. Just as the monitors around the room went insane. We all jumped to our feet as Dr. Anderson went running form the room screaming for a doctor. Everything was blur I was being

From here to forever

pushed from the room as doctors and nurses sprinted passed us.

" He squeezed my hand, he squeezed my hand. " I was screaming. They wouldn't stop they wouldn't listen. A pair of hands gripped my shoulders.

" Elizabeth you need to sit down. You need to stay calm. You have to do it for the baby sweetie. You are very high risk. We hadn't had a chance to get to that. You need to sit down right now and take some deep breaths." Dr. Anderson was leading me to a chair, sliding another one in front of me and placing my feet on it. She turned to the other three women. " I understand you are all worried. However I need you to pull it together for her. I need you to keep her calm. I will be right back. I need to get a blood pressure cuff to monitor her. Do you all understand me?" I watched them nod their heads as he turned and ran down the hall. Nan and Lilly didn't move. It was Madison who came and sat next to me. The same girl who had known Brandon as long as I had. The girl that had been both of our best friends ninety-nine percent of our lives. The girl who was pulling it together for me, when I knew she wanted nothing more then to pace. We didn't talk, it was easier that way; instead she sat with one hand on my belly, and the other gripping mine. The blood pressure cuff wrapped around my arm. I couldn't find the words to ask if my blood pressure was ok.

Without Brandon, I didn't know if I could find the strength to go on. Let alone keep myself healthy, as well as the baby. To be perfectly honest without Brandon I don't know if I want a child. How could I raise a child that would remind me daily of the person I lost? The tears finally trickled down my cheeks, as I watched more equipment rolled into his room. I wanted to get up, and pace, I wanted to scream, I wanted to throw myself on the ground and sob. But Doctor Anderson who sat holding my hand on one side and Madison holding it on the other kept me grounded. I stifled a sob as a doctor walked out into the waiting room.

" Elizabeth." He started; I was never so thankful that I was sitting down. The look on his face would have had me collapsing in a heap on the ground. " Brandon is awake an asking for you." I leapt to my feet tearing the cuff of my arm as I sprinted down the hall. I Knew he was still talking, I knew everyone else was crying, but all I cared about was hearing his voice. I couldn't believe it was true until I heard it with my own two ears.

" Brandon." I threw the door open, holding my breath. I would not survive if this was just a joke, or a dream.

"Pige." He rasp out, his blue eyes half open searching for me. I didn't stop I didn't think I closed the distance between us, and threw myself on top of him. Burring my head in his neck I breathed him in. Neither of us spoke, I just held him, basking in the fact that he was awake.

" We kinda thought there for a minute you was gonna leave us." I smiled as I quoted the Wizard Oz to him. It has always been his guilty pleasure movie.

" But I did leave you, Pige. That's just the trouble. And I tried to get back for days and days." He rasped, quoting the movie right back to me. I felt him smile against my cheek.

" But you are back now love." I whispered. I probably should let your mom come in. I started to pull away.

" She can wait, I already lost you once, and I can't bear to see you walk out that door right now." He said, the truth in his words breaking my heart. I shifted on the bed so I could lie looking at him.

" Brandon I am sorry, I am so sorry. For everything." He pressed his finger against my lips.

" You know what I think?" His eyes danced as he waited for me to respond.

From here to forever

" No." I held my breath in anticipation.

" That maybe back in high school there were things we needed to find out about ourselves before we could find each other." He leaned forward gently pressing his lips to mine, letting the end of his sentence come to rest on the tip of my lips.

" Brandon, I love you, I have always loved you. It just took me forever to figure out that you are all I am ever going to need. You are going to make an amazing father." I held my breath letting the words sink it.

" I love you to. Wait what?" He tried to sit up, struggling against his weak body.

" Brandon I am pregnant, we are having a baby. After being unresponsive for four weeks you squeezed my hand while we listened to the heart beat for the first time." He pulled me towards him pressing his lips to mine once more. A cough at the door interrupted us. I looked over and smiled as the four women who had been in the room listening with us stood in the doorway with tears in their eyes.

CHAPTER TWENTY
Elizabeth

Eight Months Later

" Ready one, two, three push." Brandon whispered in my ear. His chest pressed against my back, forcing my body forward. After twenty-seven hours of labor I was exhausted and unable to pull myself forward.

" You are almost there Iz." Dr. A urged me to keep going. She was between my legs helping the baby along. " The head is right there. Come on you can do it." I threw my head towards my chest, pushing as hard as I could. A scream escaped my lips as I pushed yet again.

"I just wanted this damn thing out now." I yelled as a shooting pain ripped thru my lower body for just a moment. Then just like that the pain was gone. My screams just as suddenly were replaced with a baby's shrill cries. A tear hit my shoulder. The love of my life weeping quietly behind me.

" You did it baby." Brandon whispered placing a kiss on my neck while chocking back more tears. I looked up to find my grandmother, Brandon's mother, Madison and even Doctor A were all wiping tears of joy off of their cheeks.

" Congratulations it's a girl." Doctor A announced, pride filling her voice as she lay my daughter on my chest. "Well Iz, have you decided on a name?" Everyone had been mad that we had refused share the sex of the baby. They were furious that we refused to even consider a name until after the baby was born. I had been terrified to jinx. I stared at the beautiful baby on my chest. Our little miracle for more then one reason. I looked over at her daddy and smiled as he freely cried.

" Hello there Hope. The whole world has been waiting to meet you." I gently kissed her head, before they whisked her away from me to clean her up.

" Hope?" Brandon asked.

" Yes Hope, I found out I was pregnant the night of your accident, and she gave me hope that you would come back to us. She brought you back to us. She is a miracle in her own right. There is not another name more fitting for such a little girl, who has accomplished so much before she even took her first breath." I squeezed his hand.

" She is beautiful." I heard all four women gush. They were the women who I knew would be permanent fixtures in her life. Hope couldn't ask for a better support system to love her, teach her, support her, and be there when she needs them the most. Madison stood with her arm around the Doctor who had quickly become a best friend to all of us. I closed my eyes as Brandon let go of my hand. I didn't need to watch him to know that he had gone to his daughter.

" This Hope is your mommy." He whispered as he carried her back over the moment the nurses were done with her. " I owe your mommy a push present, but I had to wait for you to finally make you appearance. Let me tell you little girl you certainty have made me sweat it out." I watched as he cradled her in his arm, swaying side to side.

From here to forever

" I get another present. I though she was my push present." I teased, pushing myself up in the bed. Out of the corner of my eye. I caught all four women holding their breath.

" Yes you do. In just one second. So Hope like I was saying before Mommy interrupted me. I met her in kindergarten, and she was the most beautiful thing I have ever laid eyes on. So I did what any little boy would do. I walked right up to her, pulled her pigtail, and then called her Pigeon. The nick name has stuck." He turned towards me. " I never did explain to her why I insisted on call her Pige all these years. You see in my five-year-old brain pigeons and doves were the exact same thing and doves mate for life. I knew the moment I looked at your Mommy in her cute little skirt, with her pig tails wagging back and forth that she was the person I was going to spend the rest of my life with. So Pigeon I guess this begs the question." He paused reaching into his pocket. " Will you be make me the happiest man in the world, and be my life mate. Will you marry me and make us a family?"

" Yes." Was all I could choke out before the ring box was even open. For the second time, tonight the room was full of quiet happy tears. I looked around once more overcome by the love that radiated off of the people who have come to be my family biological or non. Brandon leaned down to kiss me, and I cupped his face.

" From here until forever I will love you." I whispered into his lips, smiling at just how perfect this moment truly was.

Mandelyn Kilroy currently lives in Collegeville, PA with her cocker spaniel Chloe and her own real life Nan. She studied at Full Sail University in Winter Park, Florida. She is an avid reader, and can normally be found with a book in her hands. For more information on the author, and to stay in the know on her upcoming projects you can follower her on
Facebook https://www.facebook.com/pages/Mandelyn-Kilroy/303287943127165
Twitter https://twitter.com/mandelyn0886
Her blog http://mandelynkilroy.wordpress.com/
Or her website http://mandelynkilroy.wix.com/author

Her next novel Jane Austen Has Ruined my life is due out early fall of 2013.

There are so many people I want to thank.

Nan- Thank you for your tough love, your wisdom, your support, and above all else your love. There will never be enough words to describe just how much you have changed my life.

Dad- Thank you for cheering me on, pushing me, and for always telling me I can be anything I want to be when I grow up. Guess what that's exactly what I am doing.

Mom- Thank you for your support, your love, and for passing on your love of the written word. Also thank you for pushing me in so many ways.

To my siblings Heather, Zach, Sean, and Olivia thank you for the love you all express. Heather Thank you for being one of the first people to read this book, for believing in me when I first said I wanted to write a book, and for being my sister.. Zach Thank you for always trying to be interested in what I write, for teaching me so many life lessons, and above all else loving me. Sean thank you for

pushing me even if you didn't know you were doing it.
Stephanie- Thank you for being my gym partner, my midnight Wawa run companion, the person who understands what I mean when I can not find the right word. Thank you for being you and coming into my life as a friend only to take up residence in my heart as family. Thank you for reading this when I was afraid to publish it, and always making me laugh.

Shana - You thought I was going to forget you, not possible. You have been more then a friend for so many years now. I don't even know how to begin to thank you. Thank you for waking up in the middle of the night to listen to me rant about my characters, thank you for not committing me when I started to sound like a crazy lady. Thank you for pointing out my plot holes, my typos, and above all else being as brutally honest as possible. Thank you for loving me.

To My fellow writers Tori thank you for pushing me as I wrote this, for being your perky self, and always reminding me that the glass is half full. Thank you for talking me off the ledge when I was afraid to publish this, for loving it as much as I do, and thank you for being my NANO companion, and most of all for being a friend.

John how do I even begin to thank you. Thank you for

always reminding me that creativity can't be taught. Thank you for believing in me, for being the person I can trash talk with at 1 am (Jess I'm sorry I kept him up all those nights), most of all for being an amazing friend.

To the rest of my family who has cheered me on, read my blog, and bragged about me, Aunt Missy, Jeff, Samantha, Tiara, MaryBeth, Blaise, and everyone else I am forgetting. I love you all from the bottom of my heart.

Most of all a deep and heartfelt thank you goes out to everyone who has purchased this book, fallen in love with my characters, and recommended this book. Thank you, because of you I get to live my dream. There are not enough words to describe just how grateful I am to you. Always remember dreams aren't perfect they come true not free.

Made in the USA
Lexington, KY
26 February 2013